DAVID WEATHERLY

PALMETTO STATE MONSTERS

CRYPTIDS & LEGENDS
OF
SOUTH CAROLINA

FOREWORD BY MICAH HANKS

Eerie Lights Publishing
Eerielightspublishing.com

DAVID WEATHERLY

PALMETTO STATE MONSTERS

CRYPTIDS & LEGENDS

OF

SOUTH CAROLINA

FOREWORD BY MICAH HANKS

Based on interviews and research conducted by David Weatherly

ISBN: 978-1-945950-28-5 (Paperback)

Published by:

EERIE LIGHTS

Eerie Lights Publishing
Eerielightspublishing.com

Cover design: Sam Shearon
www.mister-sam.com

Editor: Jerry Hajewski

Book layout/design: SMAK
www.smakgraphics.com

Printed in the United States of America

Also by David Weatherly

Strange Intruders

Eerie Companions: A History of Haunted Dolls

Black Eyed Children

Silver State Monsters: Cryptids & Legends of Nevada

Copper State Monsters: Cryptids & Legends of Arizona

Monsters of the Last Frontier: Cryptids & Legends of Alaska

Monsters at the Crossroads: Cryptids & Legends of Indiana

Monsters of the Tar Heel State: Cryptids & Legends of North Carolina

Peach State Monsters: Cryptids & Legends of Georgia

Monsters of Big Sky Country: Cryptids & Legends of Montana

The Haunted Series (co-authored with Ross Allison)

Haunted Toys

Haunted Ships & Lighthouses

Haunted Churches

Haunted Prisons

Shadow Chaser (co-authored with Sean Austin)

Shadow Chaser The In-Between (co-authored with Sean Austin)

Paranormal Files: West Virginia

Wood Knocks: A Journal of Sasquatch Research

Volume One

Volume Two

Volume Three

Volume Four

Table of Contents

203
Acknowledgements

205
Bibliography

209
About the Author

PALMETTO STATE MONSTERS by David Weatherly

Foreword

Among eastern coastal states, South Carolina is unique as far as the richness of its fauna, and the plentiful paleontological and archaeological treasures its earth and sand have preserved for millennia.

Although Europeans would not arrive on its shores until the 1540s, many of the indigenous Americans who dwelt here since much earlier times lived large portions of their lives along the state's waterways. Evidence of their activities can still be found in the form of artifacts that are often recovered from the stony bottoms of rivers like the Savannah and Pee Dee, as well as their many tributaries.

Although I am not a resident of South Carolina, my love for history and learning about the past has often brought me to the numerous archaeological sites in this state, whether for independent study, or more often simply as a volunteer shoveling the sandy piedmont soil on excavations being undertaken by some of the state's finest educators and experts in their field.

Throughout the long hours I have spent digging—and sweating—in the South Carolina heat at such sites, one will occasionally hear odd stories during the banter that occurs amidst shovel scoops. I recall one instance where a group of volunteers and I were talking at a wooded site near the Savannah River one spring afternoon, when one of them suddenly said, "Hey, ask this guy to tell you about the black panther he saw!"

"Black panther?" I asked, concealing my interest somewhat, and directing my attention over to the witness. "When did you see one of those?"

The man didn't show any sign of hesitation as he told me

1

that not only once, but that on a couple of occasions he had been camping near the dig site, when right around dusk he had observed an obviously large, dark-colored cat as it darted across the unpaved road that allowed access to this otherwise remote site. In both instances, the animal was seen at a distance, but it was light enough just after sundown that he could clearly see the cat's muscular shoulders, and in particular, the thickness of its tail as it walked across the road.

"They tell us there are no panthers here," the man said, adding that black ones "aren't even supposed to exist in North America."

"But I know what I saw," he stated flatly.

On many occasions like these from over the years, I have spoken with ordinary people who say they have seen unordinary things. One aspect that is common to such experiences, however, is the conviction of the witnesses about what they say they observed. Like the volunteer archaeologist I met along the Savannah River that spring, they too know what they saw... whether or not others accept or believe it.

For my own part, it might have been easier to shrug off the man's story about a "black panther" stalking along the swampy coastal regions of some of South Carolina's most remote terrain, if not for the fact that his was similar to dozens of other stories I've collected over the years about sightings of large, black cats that have been seen here. The official position of agencies like the South Carolina Department of Natural Resources, and of organizations like the South Carolina Wildlife Federation, is that there are no remaining wild populations of the lighter colored eastern cougar found here today, and that no dark-colored variety ever existed. Although the eastern cougar is recognized as an extinct subspecies of American cougar following an official declaration by the U.S. Fish and Wildlife Service in 2018, some suggest that the northernmost ranges of the extant Florida panther could account for some scattered reports of cougar sightings. However, unlike its cousin the jaguar, *none* of the varieties of cougar in America are known to be melanistic; a trait which causes some members of the species to undergo a color morph that produces a black coloration, as opposed to the more common spotted appearance that prevails among jaguar in Central and South America.

What, then, could account for the sightings of "black panthers" that occasionally appear in South Carolina, as well as other parts of North America? Some have suggested that they could be escaped exotic pets, while others suppose that at least a few jaguars might occasionally range into the southernmost parts of North America, resulting in some of the "black panther" sightings. Whatever the source may be behind such observations, it seems evident that the situation remains unresolved.

Sightings of big cats in South Carolina, the likes of which are discussed in part four of this book, are only one variety of unusual animal that has been reported in this southeastern state. Arguably, the most famous mystery beast associated with the Palmetto State is the famous Lizard Man of Scape Ore Swamp, about which enough information has been collected that the entire second part of this collection has been devoted to it. During the 1980s when sightings of a large, bipedal creature seen in remote parts of South Carolina began to garner national attention, Scape Ore Swamp was still fairly secluded. Today, driving through the nearby town of Bishopville one will see condominiums, shopping centers, and other urbanization that appeared only in the decades since Christopher Davis first claimed he was chased along a dark country road one evening by a large creature that moved on two legs.

Some have argued that the "Lizard Man" might have been nothing of the sort and was in fact a representative (though perhaps an ugly one) of the apelike species purported to exist in various parts of North America known commonly as Sasquatch or Bigfoot. The insinuation is no less problematic, of course, since the existence of a giant species of bipedal, humanlike primate in America—or anyplace else in the world—remains unproven, and thus contested by science.

Yet the sightings persist, as they have for some time now. As researcher and master chronicler David Weatherly shows us in the present volume, sightings of creatures that match popular descriptions of Bigfoot are no recent phenomena for

South Carolinians, and have at least occurred for many decades, though perhaps even longer. An account published in July 1889 that appeared in Georgia's *Clarksville Advertiser* and was later retold in the Dunkirk, New York *Observer-Journal* describes how an indigenous resident guarding a hunting camp saw a creature that was "about seven feet high and walked erect like a man," was "hairy all over," and whose "mouth was in the chin" and possessed "great claws on the fingers and toes" as it came and stole deer from the camp one evening.

In this latest installment of his research into American states and their resident cryptids, stories like these that Weatherly presents us are merely a handful of the kinds of peculiar tales that South Carolinians have told for decades. Some of these stories, like those of Scape Ore Swamp's Lizard Man, are well known even outside of the southeast; while others like the "Thing" of '72, or the odd creatures one group of women claimed they saw in the Catawba River near Camp Canaan Island, will likely be new to many readers.

Whether they are well known stories, or among the more obscure offerings from the swamps and woodlands of the Palmetto State, each of the accounts David Weatherly provides in this volume offers a fresh perspective and will surely stoke the fires of the imagination. Many of the witnesses in these stories, like several people I have come to know during my own visits to South Carolina, claim to have had encounters with the impossible. In fact, most would probably tell you the same thing I have been told time and time again during my visits throughout the years.

They know what they saw.

—Micah Hanks

Micah Hanks is a writer, podcaster, and longtime proponent of the application of science toward the study of the unexplained. He is host of several podcasts, including Sasquatch Tracks, a program that takes a "citizen science" approach toward the mystery of Bigfoot and other relict hominoids reported in various parts of the world. You can learn more about Micah's works at his website, www.micahhanks.com

Introduction

The state of South Carolina lies in the Southeastern region of the United States. It's bordered by North Carolina on the north, Georgia to the south, and the Atlantic Ocean in the southeast.

South Carolina was one of original thirteen British colonies in America. Established in 1712 as part of the Province of Carolina, the colony was named after King Charles I of England.

Evidence of human activity in the state dates back around 40,000 years and numerous Native American tribes, including the Catawba and Cherokee, made their homes in the region.

The first European explorers were French and Spanish. Early attempts at colonies failed until an English settlement was established in the late 1600s.

The state was the first to ratify the Articles of Confederation and was an important part of the American Revolution. More Revolutionary War battles and skirmishes were fought in South Carolina than in any other state.

In December 1860, South Carolina became the first state to secede from the Union. The opening shots of the American Civil War were fired in the state when Confederate batteries shelled Union forces at Fort Sumter in Charleston Harbor in April 1861.

After the war, South Carolina was admitted back into the Union in July 1868.

South Carolina is nicknamed the Palmetto State after the state tree, the Sabal Palmetto. It's one of the nation's smaller states, coming in fortieth in size. It ranks twenty-third in population with over five million citizens as of the 2020 census. The state capital is Columbia, and the largest city is Charleston, a port city that has long been an important East Coast hub.

Textiles, agriculture, and machinery production are important parts of the state's economy and tourism has been growing consistently over the last several years with many people attracted to the state's coastal region and historic cities.

The state is divided into four regions—Upstate, Midlands, Pee Dee and Lowcountry. South Carolina also has several Sea Islands, a chain of tidal and barrier islands in the southeast portion of the state.

Overall, the climate is mostly humid subtropical with mild winters and humid summers.

Wildlife in the state includes black bear, white tailed deer, wild hogs, bobcats, and coyotes. Smaller mammals include beaver, river otters, long-tailed weasels, opossums, and the southern fox squirrel.

Birds are abundant over the state's skies from a wide range of marsh, wading, and coastal birds along the waterways to land birds in the state's interior.

Reptiles and amphibians include sea turtles, the American alligator, a wide range of frogs, toads, lizards, and salamanders, and 38 species of snake.

South Carolina's numerous lakes are home to an abundance of aquatic species including brook and rainbow trout, hickory shad, channel catfish, and American shad, and, of course, the Atlantic coast has ample sea life.

And then there are the other, unofficial creatures that are reported to wander around the Palmetto State.

Encounters with Bigfoot have been recorded from all over the state and reports include encounters as far back as the late 1800s and early 1900s.

Black panthers are reported across South Carolina. Lake Murry is said to be the home of an aggressive water monster; and legends of human-like creatures called cymbees are found in the Lowcountry.

The state's most famous cryptid, the Bishopville Lizard Man, is said to dwell deep in the mysterious Scape Ore Swamp; and while some think he came and went in a frenzy of sightings in 1988, many say he still lurks in the area.

And there's more. The state is full of strange legends, including boo hags, plat eyes, and an angry phantom dog. And then there's the University of South Carolina's creepy Third Eye Man who's said to live deep in the catacombs under the historic institution.

Welcome to a journey into the cryptids and legends of the Palmetto State.

PALMETTO STATE MONSTERS by David Weatherly

PART ONE
Weird Watery Things

Strange Things in the Water

There's a host of weird things to be found in South Carolina's waters, from early native legends to modern sightings of aquatic anomalies.

The Creek tribe mentions bizarre creatures they call the Inzignanin, a race of amphibious humanoids with a three-foot tail as thick as a man's arm and as hard as bone. By some accounts, the creatures were said to be lizard-like while other tales say they were covered in scales like a fish. By all accounts, the things had long fingers and rough or scaly skin.

The Creeks said the Inzignanin lived on a diet of raw fish and followed the waterways. Legends of the creatures go far back in tribal lore, but some say that all the Inzignanin died out.

South Carolina is, of course, known for its famous Lizard Man from Scape Ore Swamp, but long before he hit the news, another alligator creature stirred up trouble.

John LeMay dug up a report from the late 1800s detailing the Alligator Man of Palmetto Creek. LeMay discussed the tale in his book *Southerners & Saurians: Swamp Monsters, Lizard Men, and Other Curious Creatures of the Old South*. The original article appeared in the August 10, 1892, edition of California's *Woodland Daily Democrat*. The paper reports:

"The people residing along Palmetto Creek…as well as those for miles back in the slashes' are highly excited over the appearance of a strange and uncouth creature in that vicinity. The beast is described as being a creature that far outdoes the nightmare ideas of the mythologists. It is equally at home in the water, on the land, or among the tall trees of the neighborhood, where it has been most frequently seen. The general contour of the head reminds one of a gigantic serpent with this exception:

The 'snout' terminates in a bulbus [sic], monkey-faced knot, which much resembles the physiognomy of some gigantic ape. From the neck down, with the exception of some fin-shaped flippers, which extend from the arms to the waist, the creature resembles a man, only that the toes and fingers are armed with claws from two to six inches long.

"Tracks made by the beast in the soft mud around Hennis Lake have been taken to Donners Grove, where they are kept on exhibition in a druggist's showcase. Those who have seen the horn'd thing face to face say that it is a full nine feet in height, which could hardly be believed only for the fact that the tracks mentioned above are within a small fraction of fifteen inches in length. Fishermen who surprised the monster sitting silently on a mass of driftwood declared that its back looked like an alligator's, and that it had a caudal termination a yard long, which forked like the tail of a fish."

LeMay notes that the article was mostly forgotten and didn't even surface during the state's Lizard Man frenzy of the 1980s. Of course, as is typical of many stories in the 1800s, nothing more seems to have come of the Alligator Man. It is, at the least, curious, considering the state's later flap of Lizard Man sightings.

The Catawba River Runner

The 220-mile-long Catawba River is purportedly the territory of a creature called the Catawba River Runner.

The river itself originates in western North Carolina and runs all the way into South Carolina where it becomes the Wateree River, joins the Congaree River, and becomes the Santee River before it eventually empties into the Atlantic Ocean off the southeastern coast of South Carolina.

The river is named after the Catawba tribe who originally lived along the river. The natives had legends of giant snakes in the region, likely large water snakes, that lived in the river.

The Catawba River Runner seems to be mostly a local legend and there aren't a list of sightings or witnesses to confirm its existence. It is clear, however, that there has been talk of the creature, or creatures, for decades. John LeMay mentions an early ad/article from A.H. Hutchinson & Company that mentioned a water serpent:

"As the evening passenger train on the Carolina Central, which leaves Charlotte at 3:15, was passing Mt. Holly yesterday, there was great excitement as they saw a monster sea serpent in the river which looked as large around as a small hogshead, and probably thirty or forty feet long. His green serpent-like eyes were blazing like fires as he lashed the water to foam."

"Though it could sound exciting for a moment," LeMay writes, "the ending gives away the intent when it is revealed that the monster was carrying a wooden sign instructing folks to buy their livery supplies from Hutchinson's store in Charlotte."

So much for an early sighting!

One undated and often repeated sighting involves three middle school children who reportedly spotted the beast. The children, Anita Grace Gridley, Kaitlyn Hill, and Donna Shult, were out at Camp Canaan, a hundred-acre island in the river at Rock Hill. The trio saw a creature surface and, after five seconds, saw a second one come up. This time, it was a baby version of the first beast. Both creatures soon dove into the water and vanished.

There are indications that the story was fabricated, and some sources say that Anita later confessed to creating the tale.

Other purported sightings of a giant serpent in the Catawba have surfaced as recently as 2020, but the reports are unfortunately of dubious nature.

Scant reports continue about water monsters in the region and while it doesn't look good for a water monster in the river, whether or not the stories are simply fish tales or whether there's something unusual in the Catawba is still a mystery.

It is interesting to note that a damn across the Catawba River created North Carolina's Lake Norman, which is also said to be the home of a water monster named Normie, one that does come with more extensive accounts (Covered in my book *Monsters of the Tar Heel State: Cryptids & Legends of North Carolina*).

The Catawba River Runner

Pink Creature of Goose Creek Lagoon

Goose Creek Lagoon is reportedly the lair of a giant bright, salmon-pink creature with a smooth tail and short legs. The animal was spotted by naturalist Herbert Ravenal Sass around 1928. Sass and his wife were in a flat-bottomed boat when they first spotted the creature moving in the water. Sass slipped a paddle beneath the animal and lifted it up for a better look. He reported:

"It was heavy, about the thickness of a man's lower thigh, of a bright salmon pink and orange color. How long it was I don't know because both ends remained under water."

While the couple didn't get a look at the creature's head or tail, they did see a pair of legs that Sass said were similar to an alligator's or salamander's.

Sass thought the creature looked like a giant hellbender. The hellbender, also known as the hellbender salamander, is typically found in the eastern and central United States, though not in South Carolina. The December 4, 1948, edition of the *Saturday Evening Post* mentioned the animal in a brief news item under the banner "The Pink What-Is-It."

Was it a hellbender that had wound up outside of its normal range? Or was it an undiscovered population of them? As a naturalist, Sass was intrigued by the sighting and the idea of an undiscovered specimen in the Carolina swamps.

Reports state that gators have fallen from the sky in South Carolina.

Raining Animals

The December 26, 1877, edition of the *New York Times* reported an incident of alligators falling from the sky in South Carolina. The article reports:

"Dr. J.L. Smith was opening a new turpentine farm in Silverton Township. Smith said he noticed something fall from the sky and land on the ground near his tent and start to crawl away. When he closely examined the thing, he found it was an alligator. Within the next few minutes, a second alligator fell. Curiosity got the better of Dr. Smith, so he started to look around to see if he could find any more. Within the space of about two hundred yards, six more alligators were found. They were about twelve inches long and quite lively. The area where they fell is on high sandy ground about six miles north of the Savannah River. It was believed at the time that the alligators were picked up by a waterspout and deposited near Dr. Smith's tent."

In June 1901, Tillers Ferry was experiencing a heavy rainstorm. The rain itself wasn't that unusual. What the small community was stunned by were the hundreds of small fish that came down with the showers. Several types of fish—trout, perch, and catfish—all reportedly fell during the storm.

A local farmer named Charles Raley reported that after the rain stopped, there were fish swimming in the water that stood between the rows of his crops.

Fast forward to the summer of 1943, and we find that alligators were falling from the sky again. Reportedly, around July 2, heavy rainstorms started over Charleston and lasted for several days. During the course of the rain, several small alligators came down from the sky and landed on Aston Street.

The weird occurrence was repeated later in the year, December to be exact, when heavy rainstorms over Aiken County dropped a number of small gators.

In the late 1960s, heavy rains over Hemingway deposited small fish on several local farms. One girl out trying to collect eggs on her family's farm discovered the chicken yard covered with little fish.

A single gator fell during a thunderstorm on July 2, 1971. *The Charleston Evening Post* mentioned the weird anomaly in its weather almanac section on August 11, 1971.

Weird rains of things that shouldn't fall from the sky but do have been chronicled far and wide by those who collect data on strange events. It doesn't seem that South Carolina has any more than other regions, but the fact that gators have been dropped several times is certainly interesting and, of course, unusual.

Raining Animals

Early Accounts of Sea Serpents

Bernard Heuvelmans mentions an 1830 encounter with a sea monster near Charleston in his book *In the Wake of Sea Serpents*. The encounter involved the schooner the *Eagle*. The crew reportedly spotted two unusual creatures swimming around their vessel, as the book recounts:

"The captain of the *Eagle* sailed his ship to within 20-25 yards of one of the animals, then rashly shot at it with a musket. The bullet struck the creature with such force that the blow was felt by all on board. The creature apparently wasn't seriously harmed by either the bullet or the collision, however, because crewmembers saw both animals swimming off in the distance a short while later."

The ship's crew got a good look at the aquatic creatures and provided a description that stated:

"Its length was about 70 feet. The body was as thick or thicker than a 60-gallon keg, of a gray color, eel-shaped, without visible fins and apparently covered in scales, the back full of joints, or bunches, the head and beak resembling an alligator's, the former 10 feet long and as big as a hogshead."

The April 20, 1850, edition of the *Illustrated London News* recounted a story from South Carolina about the Port Royal Serpent. Reportedly, the 150-foot creature surfaced in Port Royal the previous month, on March 15. The beast was spotted in the Atlantic Ocean but entered the Broad River and continued to the swamp near Beaufort where it became stranded. Frightened residents of the area grabbed rifles and sent volleys of shot into the creature, killing it where it was. The carcass of the beast soon disappeared.

A monster reportedly appeared in the harbor at Georgetown

in the fall of 1888. The story in the October 3, 1888, edition of Orangeburg, SC's *Times and Democrat* reported on the creature under the banner "Seeing The Sea Serpent." According to the article, the monster was spotted by crew members of two ships, a tug and a schooner, on September 24. The paper recounts:

"The sea serpent is no longer a myth, a creature of overwrought imagination, but a well-established verity. A 'true-true' one was seen on last Thursday, at 3 P.M. by four persons at a point in the harbor about half-way between Georgetown and the island. Capt. A.A. Springs, of the steam tug H.L. Buck, one of the witnesses, gives your correspondent the following account:

"The tug had in tow the schooner Jesse Rosaline, on her way to the bar, and had just passed the wreck of the "Harvest Moon," which lies in the edge of the channel, when a little boy, 7 or 8 years old, son of Mr. C.W. Forster, directed his attention to something in the water over the port bow, and asked if it was a bird.

"Being in charge of the wheel, he paid little attention to the child's question, merely glancing in the direction indicated. He noticed what, at a glance, seemed to be some large bird floating in the water."

The tug continued its journey, and when it was about 200 yards from the object, Forster grabbed his glasses and examined it closer. He was able to get a good view of what he quickly realized was a creature of some kind that he said appeared to be sleeping or resting on the waves. He described the animal:

"The mouth appeared to be beak-shaped, the head oval and quite large. The body looked to be as large as a flour barrel and lay upon and in the water in the curves common to snakes while swimming.

"The tail was not, at first, entirely visible. While looking intently at the monster, something (possibly the noise of the tug) seemed to arouse it, and, in an instant, it threw its tail into the air, exposing fully fifteen feet of its length, and lashed the water into foam. It swam off in the direction of what is known as Muddy Bay and the mud flats, where it was impossible for the tug to follow. The color of the monster was very dark."

The water monster was estimated to be between thirty and fifty feet in length. The portion of its tail that lifted from the water was eight to ten inches in diameter.

The captain abord the schooner reportedly had a better view of the beast and thought it was fifty feet in length. The article speculates that the animal wasn't resting, but may have been sick:

"At the point where it was seen the water is fresh, as it is several miles below, and Capt. Springs thinks the animal was made sick by it, and if he does not find his way back to salt water very soon his life will be the forfeit for his rash visit to our port, and science may yet have an opportunity of fixing his identity."

PALMETTO STATE MONSTERS by David Weatherly

More Water Monsters

The May 13, 1870, edition of the *Morning Oregonian* reported on a "Hideous Sea Monster" that was spotted along the South Carolina coast. According to the story:

"A party coming to [Savannah, Georgia] from South Carolina through Wright River in a small sailboat manned by three oarsmen, has furnished us with a decidedly sensational account of his adventures with one of the most [indecipherable] of creatures that ever crawled or floated under the firmament of heaven, and assures us positively that he has not been deceived by any freak of fancy or undue excitement of mind.

"Our informant, on the morning of the 28th [of February], toward noon, as he tells us, was about half a mile from Wright River, a stream merging into the Savannah, two miles above Fort Pulaski, with his oarsmen pulling quietly along near the shore, when the slight built craft was suddenly and without any premonitory sign lifted up, as if by some immense roller, throwing the crew out of their seats and completely scaring the life out of them. The shock was so sudden that danger existed for a second of the boat turning over, but luckily it righted again and sank back into the water, which foamed like breakers.

"'But,' says the hero of the adventure, 'I did not heed the danger around me in this respect, nor the groveling fear of the men with me, for I could not, if my life was at stake, have taken my eyes away from the hideous creature that had caused all the commotion and was making its way lazily out of the river into the long rushes on the bank. Never before had I anticipated such a monstrosity, nor do I ever wish to see another. A creature almost indescribable, though its general appearance is fixed in my mind's eye too indelibly for pleasant afterthought.

"The beast, fish, or reptile, whatever species of God's

creation it might be classed under, was a tawny greenish color, growing more definite toward the head. The body of the creature was seal-shaped, apparently twenty feet long, and as thick as the carcass of the largest sized elephant. From this trunk sprung the most remarkable feature of the phenomenon a long, curved, swan-like neck, large enough, apparently, to have taken a man in whole, terminated by a head and jaws similar to that of an immense boa constrictor, the eyes fishy yet possessing ferocity enough in their expression to make a man tremble. The back of the beast was deeply ridged, running from the base of the neck to the extreme end of the tail, and several inches deep. An immense tail, shaped something like an alligator's, and three times longer, so it seemed, than the body, completed the tout ensemble of this wonderful anomaly. The creature navigated by feet resembling the fore feet of an alligator, and its progress on land was slow.

"'With all this combination of the terrible before me,' says our friend, 'it was not strange that I trembled, but before the frightened men had time to act, or I time to advise, the cause of our terror drew itself across the little island, out of sight, into the water beyond. It did not take us long to recover our senses, and as quickly leave the scene, though the shock to our nerves, and indeed to our belief in things possible and impossible, precluding anything like hard work.' The above statement we have from the lips of the gentleman himself, and being duly vouched for, we have every reason to believe in its truth."

My colleague John LeMay, author of *Southerners & Saurians: Swamp Monsters, Lizard Men, and Other Curious Creatures of the Old South*, is intrigued by the account and finds it believable simply due to its simplicity. The men never claimed to be attacked and there was no assertion that the creature was being sent away to some institution for study. As LeMay notes:

"The creature described sounds every bit like a plesiosaur-type creature except for the feet, which are just that and not flippers, meaning it could have been an Apatosaurus of some sort.

"Overall, he described a perfect Apatosaurus except for the alligator-like feet. An Apatosaurus had feet more akin to an elephant. However, this is only a problem if we limit the candidates to an Apatosaurus. A Nothosaurus, for example, was predominantly aquatic like a plesiosaur but had clawed, webbed feet, which a witness might compare to an alligator's from a distance. Dinosaurs from the Melanorosauridae family also had long necks with clawed feet."

It's notable that the Wright River intersects and feeds into the Catawba River, a body of water with its own monster legends as noted earlier in this chapter.

There are strange things in the Palmetto State's waters.

Colonial Lake, a tidal pond in Charleston, was the focal point of a weird story from 1902. The account, published in the *Newberry Herald and News* in its August 29 edition, claims a creature, half man, half frog, was living in the pond.

The creature purportedly appeared on the banks of the lake just before midnight one Thursday and "uttered strange and distressing cries." It remained on land for half an hour before jumping back beneath the water's surface.

A truck driver named William Harper got a good look at

the odd beast, as did an area carpenter named J.H. Thompson. Thompson said he was sitting on the east side of the lake when the monster surfaced. He described the creature to a newsman:

"The head resembled that of a huge frog, the wide, protruding eyes burning with a lurid light. It had arms and shoulders like a man, but the body tapered down like a serpent. It was covered with large, greenish scales, and I should say it was at least eight feet long from head to tail. Its mouth was filled with crooked fangs, which it snapped together with a vicious click. I do not like to remain out late at night, so I started for home soon after the thing came ashore. I can't imagine what it is, where it came from, or whether it will ever show up again. But I'm entirely satisfied with the little knowledge I have of it. I wish now I'd never seen it. I'm afraid it's going to trespass on my dreams."

The *News* reportedly sought out the expert opinion of a local Charleston man whose knowledge was "of sufficient scope to enable him to discuss the Colonial Lake mystery from the viewpoint of a scientist. The unidentified man told a reporter that the creature was "probably a megalosauria—a sub order of dinosaurian reptiles having the brain case unossified in front and no ossified alisphenoids. It has a short abdomen and an external chin. It also has deciduous scales which indicate that it is akin to the family of symbranchiate fishes. The megalosauria is almost extinct, although, according to science, it was very common in these waters forty-two million years ago."

There's little doubt that this report was a fabrication, but the bizarre nature of it is, at the least, a reflection of the folklore of the period.

Strange things still come out of the water in modern times. Sometimes, science can explain the creatures. On March 23, 2012, people at Folly Beach thought a sea monster had washed ashore when they discovered a monstrous something on the beach. The weird mass had tiny eyes, face barbs and bony, scalelike plates that gave it a bizarre appearance. Rumors flew quickly about a monster, but a veterinarian from the South Carolina aquarium cleared the matter up fairly quickly by determining that the animal was a sturgeon, a large and prehistoric-looking fish.

Another giant showed up on the end of a fishing line in 2021 when a South Carolina fisherman reeled in a massive 400-pound goliath grouper.

Newsweek ran the story of the rare catch on June 7, and reported that, in accordance with local laws, the fish had been released after it was caught. Goliath groupers were driven to near extinction in the 1990s and are still protected.

Captain Richard Pollitzer reeled the grouper in while fishing the waters of Beaufort County. "This is the first giant goliath grouper ever caught inshore in Beaufort County as far as I am aware," Pollitzer said.

"We were fishing for monster sharks and had lost a good hookup when this fish ate the bait. It didn't act like a shark, but I couldn't imagine it would be anything else. It was the last thing I expected to see come up after an hour fight."

The men on board were amazed at their catch and the crew measured it against the side of the boat. They estimated its length at seven feet five inches. The weight estimate was in the vicinity of four hundred pounds, though they had no way to weigh the fish. The goliath grouper can reach up to around eight hundred pounds in size.

The fish are not native to the county and are more typically found in the Gulf of Mexico, around the Florida Keys, and in other tropical waters. Captain Pollitzer noted that it was the first time he'd ever seen one in person.

The rare encounter goes to show that there are still many surprises below the water's surface.

Lake Murray.

The Lake Murray Monster

Lake Murray is a reservoir in the central portion of South Carolina. The lake stretches across several counties in the state—Lexington, Newberry, Saluda, and Richland—and—covers approximately 50,000 acres. It has about 650 miles of shoreline and is fed by the Saluda River. The lake is also the site of a hydroelectric power plant that was completed in 1930. The Saluda Dam was an engineering feat for its time, reaching 220 feet in height and 1.5 miles in length.

Lake Murray is a popular recreational area that includes the Dreher Island State Recreation Area. Fishing, boating, and other outdoor activities are all popular at the site.

With such a large surface area, and a maximum depth of almost 200 feet, many would say the lake is a prime spot for unusual creatures to dwell. Sure enough, shortly after the completion of the power plant, the first sighting of something strange in the lake occurred. Reportedly, residents of Irmo, a community near Lake Murray, spotted a strange creature in the water. Gilbert Little, a resident of Ballentine, was among those who said he spotted a large aquatic something in the lake in 1933. Most other reports from the period are like Gilbert's—a brief statement of something unusual and unidentified swimming around in Lake Murray.

The creature, which later became known as "Messie" in a nod to the famous Nessie of Loch Ness, Scotland, gained more attention with a dramatic encounter in 1973.

Buddy and Shirley Browning, and a friend named Kord Brazell, were out for some fishing when a large creature surfaced and made a rush toward their boat. Reportedly, the thing tried to make its way on board the vessel, but Buddy struck it with an oar, sending it back beneath the surface of the water.

The trio said the creature was about the size of an alligator, but Buddy insisted it was not a gator. All three were adamant about the thing's aggressive nature. "It tried to climb into the boat, Buddy beat it off with a paddle," Shirley reported.

None of the trio could say for sure what the creature was. "It wasn't an illusion; it wasn't an eel or sturgeon. It was unlike anything I ever saw before, and I have been fishing Lake Murray for over 20 years. We never did figure out what it was," Buddy reported.

After the encounter, Buddy rushed back to his home and retrieved his shotgun, hoping to go back and get the beast. "We were going to go back after it and claim it, but we never did see it again," he stated.

An article seven years later still referred to the trio's encounter with the creature. The September 18, 1980, edition of *The Columbia Record* out of Columbia, South Carolina, added that the boaters had reported the encounter to Joe Logan, chief of fisheries for the South Carolina Wildlife and Marine Resources Department. They told Logan the monster was "snakelike, four to five feet long with a square, mammal-like head which rises above the water as it swims with wing-like fins."

It's important to note that it was later revealed that the boaters had been drinking on the day of their sighting and many people jumped to the conclusion that because alcohol was involved, the sighting should be completely discounted. Others, however, disagree and believe that despite a few beers, the trio saw what they reported. If it were the only sighting of the lake's creature, perhaps it would be easy to dismiss, but other witnesses continued to report strange things in the water.

The Columbia Record for September 18, 1980, reports that officials believe the monster reports were simply misidentified, known animals. As Joe Logan states:

"Alligators exceeding 10 feet in length have been and are being captured in Lake Murray. It is highly probable that what fishermen have seen are alligators. For a number of years, we have transported alligators to more remote areas."

Logan notes that since they are a protected species, the

department made an effort to protect the gators and to get them away from populated areas.

"It is not common knowledge, but alligators have been numerous in Lake Murray and sightings often create fright. Imagine a dragon-like creature creeping up onto your lawn or approaching your boat."

Logan went on to tell the paper that other unusual animals had been known to show up in the lake, including seals dumped in by a prankster, and a six-foot sturgeon.

Area resident Clyde R. Lampkin of Angler's South told the paper that tales of monsters in the lake had circulated for years. Sometimes called the "Ballentine Cove Monster," Lampkin said his feelings about a potential monster were mixed.

"Someone may have dumped some ocean life into Lake Murray, and it may have mutated or crossed over the years, growing large. I hear repeatedly of strange, unidentified fish in the deep parts of Lake Murray, but until I see one, or catch one myself, I'll question their existence."

One witness who saw the creature garnered a lot of attention due to his credentials. Retired Army General Marvin Corder logged two sightings of Messie in the 1980s. The general sent a letter to the South Carolina Fish, Wildlife and Parks Department and recounted his sightings.

Corder described the animal as a "serpent-like creature 40-60 feet long with the head and body resembling a snake, with the tail of an eel."

As sightings continued to be reported, state wildlife officials continued to suggest that the creature was an alligator or large sturgeon. Witnesses, however, continued to insist that the beast was not a commonly known animal. South Carolina newspaper, *The Independent News*, described Messie as a "cross between a snake and something prehistoric," and there were enough accounts to spark the interest of some wildlife experts.

State biologist Lance Harper collected reports of the lake's monster and interviewed numerous people who had spotted the beast. Harper kept an open mind about the creature, believing that it was likely a known species that just hadn't been documented in the lake's water. Harper set nets out at locations around the lake to collect samples of fish, and something, he isn't sure what, tore gaping holes in the mesh. Of course, officials are quick to point out that this doesn't mean an unknown monster is swimming around the lake, but the holes could certainly indicate a large species like a sturgeon. The Atlantic sturgeon can grow up to nearly fifteen feet in length and reach over 800 lbs. They are often described as "prehistoric" in appearance and are known as a "living fossil."

Sightings of weird creatures in the lake increased in the late 1990s and into the early 2000s.

A 1996 report came from an anonymous caller who told radio station WNOK-FM that he'd seen something strange while fishing on the lake. The report, from October 1996, stated:

"I was fishing on Shull Island, off a friend's cover, and I saw a fin that was about two feet long come up. I thought it was a big bass, but I didn't know what it was, so I threw my line right out in front of it. It broke my rod in half and took it with it! All I had left was just the handle grip! That's all that was left. I didn't know what it was...all I know was it broke my rod in half! Just after that, I saw it roll, but that was it."

Boaters fought a water monster on Lake Murray.

In April 2000, Mary Shealey saw a weird shape in the water that resembled a capsized boat. She watched as the creature swam across the water near the Lake Murray Dam. Shealey estimated the creature's length at thirty feet while its back rose ten feet above the surface of the water.

In 2001, a woman swimming in the lake said that something brushed against her in the water. The creature had skin that was "very bumpy and sort of scaly-feeling," she said.

In 2002, a woman and her friend were driving across the dam when they spotted something they described as a "wavy, curvy, long thing" in the otherwise calm water.

Descriptions of the lake's monster continue to vary. Some say it has flippers and a long neck evocative of the Loch Ness monster. Others assert that Messie is more snakelike and massive, up to sixty feet by some accounts.

A fishing contest during the 1980 Septemberfest festival offered a one-hundred-dollar prize for the capture of the lake's monster. (The prize would be doubled if the Brownings confirmed the creature was the same as the one they had encountered). Unfortunately, no one came forward with a catch to claim the prize.

Whatever the creature is, it has continued to put in sporadic appearances through the years and locals around the lake try to take it in stride. Some shops seek to capitalize on the area's water monster by selling Messie t-shirts and other gifts. Mostly though the legend is primarily a local one, a great puzzle for those interested in such things, and a good campfire story for others. Of course, the lack of national renown doesn't mean there isn't a monster in Lake Murray's depths!

Cymbees & Mermaids

The legend of cymbees originates in western and central Africa where they were known as "simbi spirits." The Americanized spelling "cymbee" is the common one now found in the South.

Legend says that these spirits traveled with African slaves who were brought to the Americas. They are essentially territorial guardians attached to bodies of water. Any concentration of water can be home to a cymbee—streams, waterfalls, pools, ponds, even sink holes.

If a water hole suddenly dries up, it's thought to be a sign that the cymbee attached to it has died or has left due to a human offense.

Cymbees are commonly referred to as creatures that look like the common concept of a mermaid. By many accounts, they can assume full human form, though they may have webbed feet. Others state that cymbees can assume the form of a snake.

The variations may be due to differences in tribal beliefs among the African people who brought the legends with them or may be an indication that the creatures were believed to have shape shifting abilities.

Cymbees had certain powers within the waters they lived in. They could create disturbances in the water and call up high winds to make the water churn. By some accounts, cymbees would surface and cause trouble if someone tried to take any of the water from their territory.

The spiritual connection between the African people and the cymbees is of deep significance. A paper presented at the fall 2000 meeting of the Southeastern Regional Seminar in African Studies by historian Ras Michael Brown discussed the cymbees and their origins and makes note of the connection. Brown states:

"West-Central African nature deities, called simbi spirits in Kikongo, served the enslaved people of the early Lowcountry as spiritual benefactors around which captives of diverse African origins and those born in the Lowcountry built their communities.

While the cymbees had spiritual significance, they were also viewed as very real, physical entities.

Edmund Ruffin gathered stories of cymbees in South Carolina in the 1840s. On March 25, 1843, Ruffin visited Woodboo Plantation and discovered that the limestone springs in the area were referred to as fountains. Each "fountain" of any considerable size was said to be inhabited by a cymbee, and each cymbee was unique in some way. One man told Ruffin about a cymbee that was web-footed like a goose. The man hadn't seen the creature himself but had heard stories about it.

Ruffin did hear a direct testimony from a man who said he'd seen a female cymbee on a plank at one of the fountains. The plank had been laid across the water to act as a crossing point. As the man watched, the cymbee glided off the plank and vanished into the water.

According to the witness, the cymbee had long brown hair that hung down so far that it covered her face, body, and limbs. The old man told Ruffin that he was young when he'd had the sighting and at the time, it had frightened him.

Ruffin heard another story at Pooshee Plantation involving a young African boy who encountered a cymbee. The boy reported that the creature was running in circles around and around a fountain, presumably, its home.

Ruffin was told that cymbees were usually seen at night and liked to sit on low bridges or planks over the water.

When the Ravenel family enclosed a fountain on the plantation, it caused a protest among the African populace who were sure that the cymbee in the water would be offended.

Documents left by Henry Ravenel even mention the

cymbees. Ravenel believed the term was of African origin and reported that the creatures were described like a mermaid—part human female and part fish.

St. John's Parish, Berkeley County, was once rich in limestone springs and sinkholes. Henry Ravenel visited many of the springs in the area and wrote an essay in 1860 detailing his tour of the plantations in the region. The countless watery spots in the area were all said to house individual cymbees. In modern times, the area became the Santee State Park, Lake Moultrie, Lake Marion, and the Santee Canal. Most, if not all, of the springs and sink holes were lost when Lake Moultrie was created in the 1940s by a state utility project that damned the Cooper River. Did the cymbees leave, or do some still dwell in the lake?

Cymbees aren't the only human-fish hybrid creatures said to call South Carolina home. Stories of reported mermaids can also be found in the state's history.

One old legend involving a mermaid comes from the state's Sea Islands where the creature lived in an unnamed river. The story involves a man whose wife died, leaving him with a single daughter. In the tale, the man remarries, and his new wife has two daughters of her own. Rather than a happy family, the arrangement is more Cinderella like, and the new bride and her daughters treat the man's child terribly. The tormented girl soon meets not a fairy godmother, but a mermaid.

Elsie Clews Parson covers the tale in her book *Folk-Lore of the Sea Islands-South Carolina*. Parson writes:

"They treated this child very cruel. So, the first wife's daughter went to the river and began to cry. So, a mermaid rise up, and said, 'What are you crying for, my lady?'—'My mother die, and my father married again; and stepmother has two daughters, they beat me and won't give me nothing to eat.'"

The mermaid takes the girl down beneath the water and gives her a feast. When she is finished, the mermaid returns the girl to the surface. The satiated girl goes home. The family of course notices that the girl doesn't try to eat anything, and they are suspicious as to why.

The following day, the girl returns to the river and the experience is repeated with the mermaid taking her into the water and giving her plenty to eat and drink.

The mother and eldest daughter begin to wonder what the girl is up to so on the following day, the elder daughter follows her stepsister down to the river where she observes the process the girl goes through to summon the mermaid, a process which involves a song that includes the phrases:

"Thee, thee dady,

"Take me down, pretty Joe!"

The tale takes an odd and bloody twist after this. The elder daughter returns home and reports the incident to the rest of the family. They all go to the river and, after several attempts to summon the mermaid, the youngest stepsister is successful. When the mermaid surfaces expecting to find her young friend, the girl's father shoots and kills the watery creature.

As expected, the young girl soon goes back to the river and tries to summon the mermaid. None of her family members had told her that they had lured the mermaid in and killed her, so the girl thinks she's been abandoned. In despair, she enters the water and drowns herself.

This grim account is a curious piece of lore but it's not the only instance of mermaids in the Palmetto State's history.

Nancy Rhyne, author of *Tales of the South Carolina Low Country*, mentions mermaid lore in her book. The brief note is listed as having come from a Dr. J. Ward Flagg. It states:

"From the moment a sea maiden is taken from her native environment, a storm builds in the West Indies. Vicious, gaining momentum, the gale follows a path to Murrells Inlet, a village under moss-draped oaks. If the mermaid is not released from captivity by the time the storm reaches the Inlet, winds unleash their energy and great rods of lightning seem braced by struts of fire. The rains come faster and faster, and the water level rises until the mermaid is washed back to her home in the Atlantic."

Purportedly, after the storm, an "unearthly pink glow" illuminates the landscape, highlighting the destruction wrought by the elements. An even more dramatic story involving a mermaid and a storm is a well-known tale in the Charleston area and has been repeated for many years.

Reportedly, stories of mermaids being seen in Charleston Harbor date back to the 1700s. While intriguing, there are few if any actual accounts to be found involving encounters with the creatures so this could simply be part of local lore, but one particular mermaid legend has been around for decades. It's commonly known from John Bennett's 1943 book *Doctor to the Dead: Grotesque Legends and Folk Tales of Old Charleston*. The story appeared in the book under the title *The Apothecary and the Mermaid*.

According to Bennett, the story took place in July 1867, and it began with rain.

On July 3, a heavy squall moved across the city, followed by drenching rain. Around midday, the rain grew stronger; driving sheets of it fell without interruption. The rain continued for weeks. Day and night it came down, so much so that it transformed the city. Bennett describes the conditions created by the unceasing downpour:

"The sky seemed truly to have burst, the rain streamed down in torrents, the countryside was inundated, the lowlands swamped the roads underwater, and still, with ever increasing force, the unabated rain poured down. The sodden woodlands rotted, dripped, and stank; the mire in the city streets was ankle deep everywhere; in deeper puddles half knee-deep the sandy roads were slop; all that was not geological rock or oystershell was muck.

"Cockroaches flooded from their holes under the low-slung houses, swarmed into the streets by the thousands and were drowning among the cobbles; drowned cats floated in the streets, dead rats, washed out of the wharves below the cotton compresses, came bubbling up the street drains from the bay."

Of course, all of this added to the miserable conditions that people in the city were already suffering due to the onslaught of rain. Water flooded into homes, down the chimneys, and up from the streets. Roofs leaked, floors oozed with water, storm sewers failed, unable to handle such large quantities of rain. The eastern side of King Street collapsed and getting anywhere was fraught with challenges.

It should come as no surprise that under such conditions people grew uneasy and fearful. Surely, some thought, there must be a supernatural explanation behind what was occurring in the city. Perhaps a deity or some supernatural force was angry.

Soon, an answer was presented. It reportedly came from an old woman who wandered the streets telling the populace that within the city, a mermaid was being held captive. Until she was released back into the sea, the woman said, the rains would continue.

With people suffering and looking for answers, they listened to the old woman and her prediction quickly spread around the city. Soon, an angry mob began to form. They were determined to find the mermaid and take her back to the ocean so the city could be freed from the driving rain.

The mob's attention was soon focused on one particular location—the Apothecary of Dr. Trott. According to Bennett, Trott ran not just an apothecary, but a shop that also contained a museum of oddities. Bennett writes that Trott had amassed the collection for scientific reasons, or perhaps just for curiosity, and had:

"Collected in spirits of wine, an uncanny museum of untimely deaths, queer creatures, and malignant things to which poor human flesh is heir, and had sequestered them in a small stockroom at the rear of the prescription desk, beyond the wooden grille...wretched remnants of aborted things, plucked away from untimely limbo by the hand of Death, human deficiencies and deformities, and dried things under bell glasses."

Such a shop garnered enough attention on its own, but during the raging downpour of rain, the strangeness of the place quickly became a focal point when Trott's porter, Isaac Tucker, told a couple of friends about one of Trott's special displays.

On a top shelf in the apothecary, Tucker claimed, was a glass jar with pale green water that held a mermaid.

The creature was tiny, only a span in size (a span is the distance from the tip of one's thumb to the tip of the little finger). The mermaid had flowing locks of yellow hair and around her in the glass swam two goldfish.

Once the growing mob got wind of the story, they began to converge on Trott's shop, looking to free the mermaid. Once the mob made its way to Trott's shop, they began to batter it with rocks, stones, clumps of mud, anything they could find. They broke the windows and beat on the doors and shutters, all the while demanding that the mermaid be brought out and set free.

Trott appeared at an upper window of the shop, assuring the crowd that there was no mermaid inside. The mob refused to believe him and people in the street grew angrier. They began trying to force their way in, hoping to find the mermaid and take her back to the ocean.

Finally, several men of the gentry class were able to enter the shop through a western window. They addressed the crowd below from an upper window and tried to get them to disperse, but the mob would not calm down.

Finally, the men said they would search the shop

themselves, along with three men chosen from the mob as representatives. William Holmes, Joe Cole, and a fellow known as Old Man Rutter were called forth. Together, the men made a thorough search of Trott's premises.

No trace of a mermaid was found. To be sure, the men searched the shop again to no avail.

When they had completed their task, several of the men went out on the roof and reported their findings to the gathered crowd.

"There is no mermaid here, upon our word of honor. Go to your homes and keep the peace, or the army must be called to disperse you."

At that moment, the rain stopped.

The stunned crowd began to filter away and the sun finally came out, shining brightly on the city of Charleston.

Was a mermaid once held captive in Charleston?

If the mermaid wasn't there, and hadn't been freed, how had the rain stopped, some wondered.

Years later, a woman named Eliza Burns recounted the excitement of the period. She was a young girl at the time and recalled hearing that some fishermen had captured a mermaid in their nets and brought it ashore and that it was being held in Trott's shop.

Burns went to see if she could get a look at the creature but found the mob so dense that she couldn't even get close. As she recalls:

"I could get no closer than High Battery and Water Street. I came down two days to see. The second day something had happened; they said that the mermaid was dead. If she was dead, they should have exhibited her and charged ten cents apiece to see. I do not know; there was a smell like something dampish and spoiled; they said it was the mermaid."

Stories about the sea creature continued to be part of the tale of Charleston's deluge. Some said that the mermaid was still there, hidden away in a glass jar on the back of a shelf in the shop.

Others believed that being out of her native sea water had caused the mermaid to shrink and become unrecognizable.

Perhaps, some said, Dr. Trott had secretly released her.

Whatever the case, it's said that the streets around the apothecary reeked of a singular, fishlike smell for days after the event.

As for Dr. Trott, he sold his shop and left the country, setting up on foreign shores where it's said he died soon after.

A few historic notes: While the story is commonly known from Bennett's *Doctor to the Dead*, he first mentioned the tale in an earlier book, with the 1906 title *The Treasure of Peyre Gaillard Being an Account of the Recovery, on a South Carolina Plantation of a Treasure*. The book talked about the "Mermaid Riot" that had occurred in Charleston. After the title was published, Bennett received some criticism on the veracity of the story, enough that he wrote to the press to clarify his source for the tale. The January 22, 1907, edition of Chillicothe, Ohio's *Chillicothe Gazette* is one of the papers that printed the story. Bennett reports that he heard the account from Araminta Tucker, a Charleston nurse. The woman had a direct connection to the tale. She told Bennett that her son-in-law had worked for Dr. Trott during the time of the riots.

Tucker's testimony, printed in the paper, adds some additional and contradictory details to the story. Notably, the woman reports that the incident took place "before the war." Other facts in the article specify the date as the summer of 1853.

Tucker also reports that the mermaid was kept in a tub of water in the cellar, implying that the creature was a human-sized specimen. She also notes that stories circulated that the mermaid had lovers on land that she had followed ashore.

Tucker says that the unceasing rain led to people filing a complaint with the city to demand the release of the mermaid. According to her, the city did in fact demand that Trott return the mermaid to the ocean, and he complied, thinking it better to release the creature before he had additional problems.

This version of the account is interesting since it is closer to the source material, having come directly from someone present at the time of the incident. It also gives us a picture that the mermaid was human-sized and closer to our common, folkloric depictions of the creatures rather than the more common story about a diminutive specimen that was kept in a jar on a shelf. The later story may have arisen due to the tales of the creature shrinking or may been inspired by P.T. Barnum's famous Fiji Mermaid.

Untangling a story like the legend of the Mermaid Riot is never an easy task When folklore and fact dovetail into a story that gets told and retold countless times, much can be lost in the resulting muddle. Given the facts, however, it seems clear that Bennett either forgot some of the details or took creative license by the time he rewrote the story for *Doctor to the Dead*.

As to whether or not Dr. Trott really had a mermaid, or something akin to it, in his basement, well, that's a mystery that we can't really solve at this point. For the mass of citizens that believed the story, it was a reality, and the strange moment when the rain ended convinced them of their truth.

Cymbees & Mermaids

PALMETTO STATE MONSTERS by David Weatherly

PART TWO
The Bishopville Lizard Man

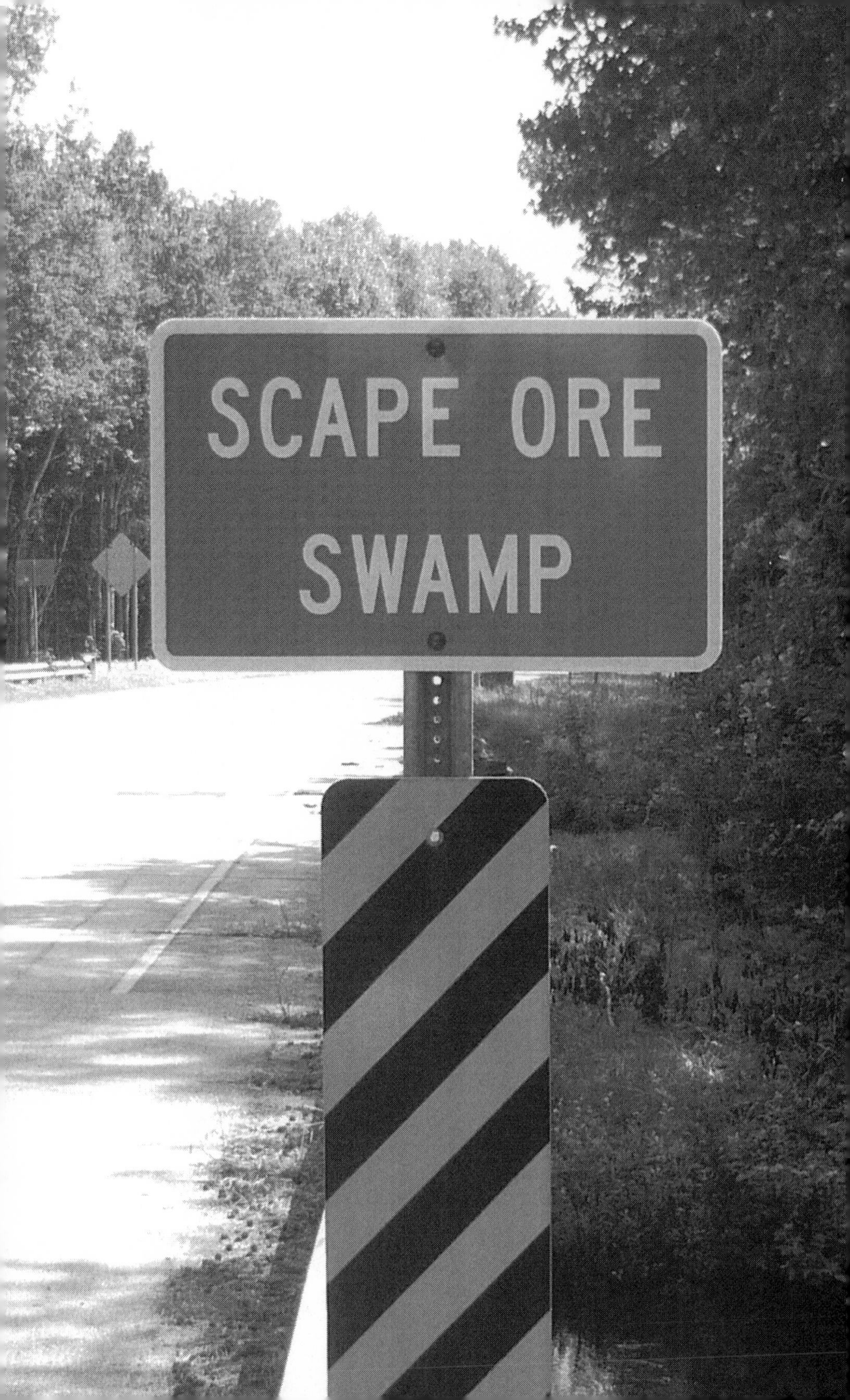
SCAPE ORE
SWAMP

Bishopville and Its Monster

Bishopville is a small town of just over three thousand people and is the county seat of Lee County. Historically, Lee County was known as the state's leader in cotton production, but in modern times, the county, and Bishopville in particular, is known for something more unique—its monster—the Lizard Man.

Reportedly, stories of the creature circulated for some time on the outskirts of Bishopville. The tales were centered around the community of Browntown and the mysterious Scape Ore Swamp which it bordered. But as often happens with monster stories, the real frenzy began when newspapers got hold of the tale and put it out for public consumption.

On the morning of July 14, 1988, an unusual call came into the Lee County Sheriff's office. Browntown residents Tom and Mary Waye wanted to file a report of vandalism. In the middle of the night, they reported, their 1985 Ford LTD had been torn up and received extensive damage, but it didn't appear to be damage done by humans, rather, the Wayes said the car had been "mauled" by something.

The Wayes car had been parked at their home under a metal carport. The physical damage to the vehicle was clear, and there was bizarre evidence that seemed to indicate the culprit was an animal. Hair and muddy footprints around and on the vehicle pointed to something non-human. The puzzling question was, what animal would maul a car and why?

Two deputies were dispatched to inspect the damage and when they arrived at the Waye home, they found a weird scene. Just like the Wayes had reported, the vehicle had been mauled. The sidewalls were scratched and dented, the chrome trim was torn away from the fenders, and the hood ornament was broken. The antenna was also bent, and wires had been yanked out from the motor. Stranger still, the deputies saw what looked like teeth marks on parts of the chrome trim, indicating that something had bitten the metal.

As the officers took in the scene, they examined the muddy footprints on the vehicle and noticed clumps of reddish colored hair that had been left behind. The scene was so strange that the deputies decided to call Lee County Sheriff Liston Truesdale. Truesdale was a veteran lawman and had been appointed sheriff of Lee County in 1974. The deputies thought that Truesdale might be able to determine what had happened to the vehicle.

Sheriff Truesdale soon arrived at the Waye home and inspected the vandalism himself. He interviewed the family and believed they were being honest with what they reported. The sheriff agreed that it looked like an animal had caused the damage, but it was difficult to determine what kind of animal was involved. Truesdale called on a biologist with the South Carolina Wildlife and Marine Resources Department. The biologist thought the hair fibers were from a red fox but was at a loss to explain the extensive damage to the vehicle. Hair was collected and sent to the University of Georgia for examination.

While it seemed clear that some of the tracks around the Waye home were from a fox, there were other prints that were more difficult to identify. About twenty-five yards from the Wayes' car were larger tracks that led to the swamp. The prints appeared to be from a large biped or quadruped and there was speculation that they were made by a bear. Black bear have been known to turn up in Scape Ore Swamp, but again, the collection of evidence was odd and disconnected. If a fox hadn't attacked the car, was it a bear? Were the two of them in it together?

Beyond that, some people didn't think the tracks near the swamp were from a bear at all since the trail seemed to be in a straight procession, like a human's trail would be.

The presence of law enforcement at the Waye house had attracted attention. People from around the neighborhood gathered to see what was happening and the call over the police scanner had attracted a few reporters. One reporter, Jan Tuten, a writer for Sumter's *The State* newspaper, was riding with Sheriff Truesdale that day.

The officers went to work dispersing the crowd and it was during this time that another possible culprit was mentioned by locals—a seven-foot-tall, red-eyed creature that was said to live in the nearby swamp. As if the puzzle weren't complicated enough, now there was a purported monster in the mix! Truesdale and the deputies probably would have dismissed the talk, but locals were insistent that the thing was real, and that numerous people had encountered it.

My colleague Lyle Blackburn investigated the Lizard Man case in depth and interviewed Sheriff Truesdale about the case. (Truesdale passed away in 2015, a couple of years after Blackburn interviewed him.) Truesdale indicated that the Waye incident is what set off the use of the Lizard Man moniker to describe the beast. As Blackburn recounts in *Lizard Man: The True Story of the Bishopville Monster*, the sheriff was leaving the scene when he by chance spotted a familiar face:

"'I saw a guy that I knew by the name of J.J.,' Truesdale recalled. 'I said, J.J., have you heard anything about a tall creature, possibly green with big red eyes?' He said, 'What, do you mean, that *Lizard Man*?' And that's how we first heard of it."

Obviously, the reporter liked the sound of the creature's name and soon it hit the papers. As Blackburn writes, "It was a simple name, but one that conjured an array of wild mental images."

Wild indeed. And in short order, the Lizard Man legend was going to get even wilder.

The Davis Encounter

Two weeks prior to the Wayes' car being mauled, another incident had occurred that proved to be even stranger, but the information would not come out until after the tale of the Wayes' damaged vehicle was published in the paper.

It was June 29, 1988. Seventeen-year-old Christopher Davis had worked the night shift at McDonald's and was finally on his way home. Driving on Browntown Road at about 2:30 a.m., he heard a noise and felt a sudden trembling in his car's steering wheel indicating a dreaded flat tire.

He was still around seven miles from his house, too far to walk, so he gritted his teeth, popped the trunk, and went about the chore of changing the tire. The young man finished his task, closed the trunk and was ready to resume his journey when he heard a thump behind him. He turned around to see something that terrified him. A figure was in a nearby field, running toward him. As reported in the August 2, 1988, edition of the *Charlotte Observer*, Davis stated:

"The moonlight was out. I turned around and saw a red-eyed devil. He was about 30 yards from me, in the field. It had real long arms. When he would run, his arms would swing."

With the thing coming toward him, Davis quickly jumped into his car for safety. But the creature wasn't deterred by the boy being inside a vehicle. Davis continues:

"I ran to the driver's side and got in. When I was sitting in the car, I saw him from the neck down. I pulled off, and after about 2 yards he jumped on the roof. I saw hands, rough-looking, black-fingernailed hands. After he jumped on the car, he grunted. A deep grunt. He grunted one more time."

Davis saw the creature's hands through the windshield

61

where they curled around the roof as the thing held on to the boy's vehicle. It was enough to spur him to further action. He turned over the engine and hit the gas. The car sped forward and the sudden motion caused the creature to tumble off. But the encounter wasn't over. The creature got up quickly and pursued the vehicle. Davis estimated that he was going about 35 mph when the thing caught up. It leapt at the car and Chris heard a loud sound when it landed on the roof.

By this time, the young man was truly terrified. He started to swerve the car, hoping to shake the monster off the top as he sped down the road. Although he didn't hear the thing fall off, his tactic seemed to work because the banging and clawing sounds on top of the car stopped.

He sped the rest of the way home, pulling into the driveway and blowing the horn as he jumped out and ran into the house.

Chris's father had heard the arrival and saw his son rush in, clearly in a state of panic. The young man was so upset and anxious to get inside that he had left the car's engine running.

After a few moments, Chris started crying. Once he calmed down enough, he told his father about the encounter.

Mr. Davis went out to check the car. The driver's side mirror was bent and twisted and there were scratch marks on the roof. As strange as the story was, Mr. Davis knew that something unusual had happened to his son and he was sure the boy wasn't making the story up.

Chris's father, Tommy, was a practical man. He'd spent years working for a plant in Sumter where he was head of the electrical department. Two weeks after his son's incident, he learned that Chris wasn't the only one in the area who'd had their vehicle damaged by something strange. Tommy read an article in the local newspaper about the weird damage on the Wayes' car. He decided that it was time for him and his son to pay a visit to the Lee County Sheriff's Office.

Truesdale listened carefully to Chris Davis's story, and, despite how outrageous it seemed, he believed the young man was telling the truth. Chris told the sheriff that he'd heard stories about a strange creature in the area going back two years. To his credit, Davis didn't dismiss the possibility that he'd seen a bear, one that was wet and covered with mud, but just like in the Waye incident, the actions didn't indicate the typical, known behavior of a bear.

The sheriff asked the Davis men if they would be willing to take a lie detector test, and both readily agreed. Truesdale agreed to set up the test and the men left. (Christopher Davis later took and passed the polygraph test.)

Investigating a possible Lizard Man must have been the most bizarre thing the sheriff had ever dealt with in his career. But, as he told Blackburn, there's wasn't a lot of choice at the time:

"We had to keep looking into the situation at that point. If it turned out to be nothing, then fine. But if it turned out to be something dangerous, then we would've been in real trouble if we hadn't done something about it."

The Lizard Man once dominated South Carolina news.

The Monster Hunt Unfolds

News reports about Chris Davis's encounter was the tip of the iceberg in terms of media attention. In short order, Bishopville radio station WAGS-AM joined in by talking about the Lizard Man on air. Station owner Emory Bedenbaugh, who'd heard about the creature from Deputy Chester Lightly, called in the big media guns by alerting the South Carolina News Network, the Associated Press, and the United Press International.

Suddenly, Browntown Road became crowded with curiosity seekers and monster hunters. Around the clock, there was a nonstop flow of traffic along the route as people searched for signs of the creature. But things were about to get even more out of hand.

Columbia, SC, radio station WCOS-FM announced a million-dollar prize for anyone who could bring the Lizard Man, or "lizard thing" as they called it, in alive.

The hordes of people arriving in Bishopville increased, and now, many of them came with guns. Along with those hoping to bag the monster and cash in, there were television reporters, photographers, and newsmen. TV crews shot footage, interviewed locals, and hoped for a golden shot of the monster, or at least something strange they could present to their viewers.

For area officials, it was bad enough dealing with the influx of people, but with the sudden media attention, the Lee County Sheriff's Department was overwhelmed with questions and phone calls. For the press, the story was new and fresh, and they were anxiously awaiting the next development. It soon came.

On July 24, a pair of teenagers burst into the sheriff's office at around two in the morning. They were clearly distressed and asked to speak to an officer. Deputy Wayne Atkinson stepped forward to see what the problem was. Right away, they told the officer they thought they'd seen the Lizard Man.

Atkinson calmed the boys down and asked them to tell him exactly what had happened. The two teens, Rodney Nolf and Shane Stokes, told the deputy that they had been driving along Highway 15 with their girlfriends when a large animal on two legs ran across the road in front of their vehicle. The creature had jumped a fence and vanished into the woods.

A few hours after Nolf and Stokes had reported their sighting, a Browntown resident called the station to report strange howls from the woods near his home.

With the report from the two teenage boys combined with the call about unusual howls, and the ongoing Lizard Man frenzy, Atkinson decided he should drive over to the area and see what was going on. State Trooper Mike Hodge was on duty that night and Atkinson got him to ride along.

The men cruised around Browntown, using a spotlight to scan the area looking for anything unusual. When they reached Bramlette Road, they spotted a number of 40-gallon drums scattered along the road along with other garbage. Getting out to investigate the area further, they found several anomalies; the drums appeared to have been crushed and trees around the area had branches that had been snapped—nine feet overhead. As if the scene weren't eerie enough, the officers had the unnerving feeling that they were being watched. Considering that there were heavy woods on both sides of the road, it would have been easy for someone, or something, to watch the officers from cover.

Atkinson and Hodge decided that the drums had either been dumped intentionally or had fallen off a truck. They returned to their vehicle and continued down the road to see if there were any other disturbances. Finding nothing, they made a U-turn and drove by the scattered cans again. This time, they noticed something else at the scene—a set of footprints that crossed the road. This was all the more unsettling considering that the footprints had not been there moments before when they investigated the area!

The officers got out to inspect the trackway. They found prints measuring 14 inches in length at the widest portion and 7 inches across. The creature's stride was over three feet with each step. Examining the tracks closely, the men saw clear impressions of a large palm pad, heel, and three claw-like toes. And the creature was apparently heavy. The tracks sank about an inch and a half into the ground. This was all the more impressive because the ground was hard, packed dirt. The men followed the tracks until the trail went into the thick brush. Given the conditions, and unsure what they were dealing with, they decided to wait until daylight to investigate further.

The Rock Hill Herald spoke with officer Hodge about the incident. As reported in the paper's July 28, 1988, edition, Hodge was puzzled by the tracks:

"I was pretty spooked. They were just some weird tracks. They were too consistent to be fake. They were deep down in that hard dirt."

Atkinson and Hodge called Sheriff Truesdale to the scene on Bramlette Road. The sheriff was also puzzled by the tracks. With the Lizard Man craze sweeping the area, he suspected a hoax, but he just couldn't figure out how the tracks had been made if that were the case.

Truesdale called on the State Law Enforcement Division and requested bloodhounds be sent to the scene so they could follow the tracks into the brush. He also sent one of his men for plaster so they could make plaster castings of the prints.

Truesdale had directed his men to block the road off so they could investigate the area, but it didn't stop reporters from showing up anyway. The sheriff had already agreed to an interview with Fox TV, and now a crew from CNN appeared at the roadblock wanting to do a story on the Lizard Man.

Truesdale put the reporters on hold while the officers finished investigating the scene. Deputies set about making plaster casts of the prints while storm clouds rumbled overhead.

Three wildlife officials from the State Law Enforcement

Division arrived with a team of bloodhounds. The trio took a look at the tracks and none of them believed they were from an actual creature. Nevertheless, they put the dogs to their task of following the trail to see what they could find. The animals had a hard time picking up the scent, and once they entered the brush, the tracks became much harder to see. By the time they were 150 yards into the swamp, the storm clouds let loose, and the hunt had to be stopped due to the pouring rain.

Cast of the Lizard Man's track.

Truesdale's men had been able to make castings of five prints before the rain came. The whole incident remained a puzzle, but at the same time, the convenience of finding large, bipedal, lizard like tracks in the midst of the Lizard Man craze was a bit too much to believe. The biggest concern, however, was the growing danger of someone getting hurt because of the ongoing monster hunt.

Scape Ore Swamp held many dangers all on its own—snakes, sink holes, and other hazards—but by adding in armed, would-be monster hunters, the combination was very concerning.

In the weeks following the scene on Bramlette Road, rumors and tales continued to circulate but no solid evidence of the creature surfaced. The next significant reports were actually old accounts that turned up due to the sheriff's continuing investigation into the matter.

A thirty-one-year-old resident of Browntown came forward and shared his story with Truesdale. The man, George Holloman, was a construction worker who said he'd had a frightening experience the previous October near the Scape Ore Bridge.

Holloman reported he had been riding his bike late one night in early October. Around midnight, he stopped at a natural artesian well on the south side of the Scape Ore Bridge. He drank some water from the well, lit a cigarette and stood enjoying the cool night air. As he was gazing around, he spotted what he first thought was a tree that had been struck by lightning. He stared at the object and was shocked when the "tree" moved.

Suddenly, whatever it was stood up on two legs. The shape was manlike, seven to eight feet tall, black in color, and staring straight at Holloman. The man dropped his cigarette and stood frozen to the spot as the thing stared at him. The scene shifted when an approaching car broke the silence and its headlights reflected the creature's eyes, causing them to glow eerily. Holloman said the eyes were large and red.

Apparently startled by the vehicle, the creature took off into the swamp, and Holloman, wasting no time, got on his bike, and headed in the opposite direction, peddling as fast as he could until he reached his home.

Another account that surfaced was the experience of George Plyler. Like Holloman, Plyler had kept quiet about his experience but finally came forward and spoke to Sheriff Truesdale about the area's creature.

Plyler said that his encounter had taken place in the spring of 1986. Plyler and a crew of three men were working near his home on Springvale Road at the boggy bottoms of Scape Ore Swamp. The men were putting up a hog pen when Plyler had the weird feeling that he was being watched. He looked around and spotted what he first thought was a deer peering out from behind a tree. He quickly realized it wasn't a deer at all. Plyler couldn't figure out what the thing was. He saw a human shaped face, round eyes, and arms that hung down like an ape's would.

The creature stared at Plyler from around the tree trunk for a few moments, then took off running on two legs, disappearing into the swamp.

Plyler was later interviewed on an episode of *Animal X: Natural Mystery Unit*, an Australian production that examined cryptological mysteries. In the episode, Plyler recalled:

"The features were more like a human than any animal I've ever seen. The arms were a little bit longer than normal human-being arms, but the legs were long and skinny, along with a little body. It had a body similar to a lizard except for the head, and it didn't have a tail or anything like that."

Another twist in the Lizard Man saga came on August 6, 1988, when an airman stationed at Shaw Air Force Base thirty miles south of Bishopville reported his encounter with the creature.

Kenneth Orr said that he was traveling to the base at six a.m. on August 5 when he saw the beast. Orr said he exited Interstate 20 onto Highway 15 and that when he got close to Gin Branch Road, he saw a creature running down the embankment.

Orr said the thing was green with a "lizard-like tail," and was approximately 5 feet 9 inches tall. According to the airman, the thing ran across the highway, then made a loop and headed for his vehicle. He pulled out his .357 Magnum, shouted at the creature to halt, and fired a warning shot. When the thing continued toward him, the man shot it several times. Orr claimed one of the shots hit the creature in the neck, causing it to falter and lean against the car for support. It gained its balance and retreated into the nearby woods.

Orr used a napkin and collected blood and tissue samples that had been left on the hood of his car where the creature had leaned. He turned the samples over to the authorities, along with a drawing he'd made of the creature, a drawing that looked like a bipedal alligator, complete with a long tail.

The account was a dramatic one, and even included physical evidence, but Sheriff Truesdale didn't believe it for a moment. The sheriff recognized the physical evidence as fish scales, and there were other factors about Orr that didn't sit well. The man drove a camouflaged Toyota with fake machine guns on it. Not a crime, but a reflection of the man's personality at the least.

Orr left the station sticking to his story, but Truesdale was getting fed up with some of the craziness that the Lizard Man had brought to town.

As it turned out, Kenneth Orr didn't have a permit for his .357. When deputy Bill Moore walked outside to look Orr's vehicle over, he saw the gun lying on the passenger seat. Truesdale decided to issue a warrant for Orr. Carrying without a permit came with a hefty fine and possible jail time.

Orr returned to the station on August 12 and admitted that he had hoaxed his Lizard Man encounter. He told officials that he did it because he wanted to keep the legend alive.

Another Lizard Man account that was more believable came from a local cropduster named Frank Mitchell.

Mitchell worked for local farms for years dropping fertilizer on fields of cotton and corn. His strange sighting occurred during the Lizard Man flap of '88, about a month or so prior to Chris Davis's encounter.

On the morning of his sighting, Mitchell had been delayed in taking off due to heavy fog. Once the weather cleared, he climbed in his plane and started down the runway. Mitchell told Lyle Blackburn what happened next:

"I got down the runway, at the point I had to take off, and that's when this *thing* just walked across the runway right in front of me. But it didn't run; it kinda had a lope in its walk as it came across the runway and just looked at the airplane.

"I couldn't tell if it was scaly or hairy, but it was a grayish-brown thing with a face like a monkey."

Once he was airborne, Mitchell made a turn and flew back over where the creature had been, but it was gone, vanished into the thick trees on the opposite side of the airstrip.

On August 26, 1988, Robert Cooper, an officer in the Army Corps of Engineers, was traveling along McDuffy Road in the Ashwood Section of Lee County when he had a strange encounter.

Cooper and his wife had attended a wedding rehearsal and were on their way home. Cooper rounded a curve near Ashwood Lake and saw a large creature step out of the darkness and dart across the road. Cooper was quoted in the August 31, 1988, edition of the *Lee County Observer* as reporting that the thing was "about eight feet tall with a tail that did not quite reach the ground."

Cooper's wife was sleeping, and he called out to her to rouse her. She sat up just in time to see the creature as it ran off the road and vanished into the trees. Cooper slowed down, hoping to get a better look at the thing, but he elected not to stop to investigate further. A practical man, Cooper says he never thought much of the Lizard Man reports that had surfaced in the area. Still, his sighting was so bizarre that he felt the need to report it to authorities.

Truesdale spoke with the man and took the report. Initially, Cooper's name was withheld from the public, but eventually his identity was revealed.

Sheriff Liston Truesdale.

The Lizard Man Lingers

The media's fascination with the Lizard Man soon waned. With no other sightings reported, things in Lee County slowly returned to a more normal state. It was two years after the Cooper report that another sighting was reported to officials.

On July 30, 1990, Bertha Blythers and her five children had been out to eat in Bishopville and were on their way back to their home in Camden. Traveling west on Browntown Road, Bertha and her kids were having a good time eating and talking. At around 10:30 p.m., Bertha crossed over the Interstate and was nearing the intersection of Hickory Hill Road when a large figure appeared and leapt toward the passenger side of the vehicle.

Bertha's oldest daughter, eleven-year-old Tamacia, was sitting in the passenger seat with the window down. When she spotted the creature, the girl screamed. In a panic, Bertha swerved the car away from the thing. She later told the police:

"I saw this big brown thing. It jumped up at the window. I quickly sped up and went on the other side of the road to keep him from dragging my 11-year-old girl out of the car."

Bertha's son, eighteen-year-old Johnny, looked back and told his mother that the creature was still there. It was walking on two legs and was only visible a few seconds before it vanished into the darkness.

Bertha told officials with the Lee County Sheriff's Office that the creature was tall, wide and had two arms like a human. The entire thing happened so fast that Bertha wasn't able to get a look at the creature's face or any further details.

Johnny agreed with his mother about the creature's appearance, adding that it was covered in brown hair, had large eyes, and was six feet tall or better.

Bertha called the sheriff's department to report the incident, and the following day, she, Johnny and Tamacia all went down and filed an official report with Sheriff Truesdale.

None of the witnesses thought that what they had seen was human, but they were at a loss to explain exactly what it was.

The next significant report involving the creature didn't come for another two years.

In May 1992, Brian and Michelle Elmore told Sheriff Truesdale that they had almost collided with a large, gorilla-like animal on Browntown Road the previous year.

The Elmores, both in their twenties, were locals and were well familiar with all the Lizard Man talk. They had held off sharing their story because they were concerned about ridicule, but they had finally decided to share the details with Truesdale.

The Elmores said their encounter had taken place in the fall of 1991 when they were on their way to a late-night party. It was about 12:30 a.m. and the couple were driving along Gum Springs, a route that connects the communities of Browntown and Cedar Creek.

Brian saw something on the side of the road that caught his attention. At first, it looked like an animal that was crouching or hunched over, but it stood upright. Startled, Brian asked his wife if she had seen the thing and she confirmed that she had. The couple bantered for a moment about what the creature was, and Brian turned the car around to get another look.

When the lights hit the creature, it darted out and ran in front of the vehicle, then into the woods.

Brian reported that the creature resembled a gorilla but was much larger than any gorillas he had seen. It was bipedal, had long arms and legs, and ran in a "humped over" position, he told Truesdale.

Michelle's statement aligned with her husband's report. She added that the creature was around seven feet tall and brown to black in color.

While the Blythers and Elmore accounts were fascinating, they didn't capture the attention that had peaked during the summer of 1988's Lizard Man craze.

Things became quiet in Bishopville, and for a time, the Lizard Man remained a curious local legend that people still talked about over cups of coffee or evening drinks.

Had the monster left the area, or had it retreated deep into Scape Ore Swamp?

A weird incident in 2008 had people questioning whether the Lizard Man had returned. On the morning of February 28, Bishopville resident Bob Rawson walked outside and found that his Dodge Grand Caravan had been mauled during the night. The damage was heavy. There were chunks missing from the hood, the grill had been punctured, and both fenders were scratched up and bent. There were what looked like teeth and chew marks in the metal and there was blood on both the front and side of the van.

Bob and his wife, Dixie, surveyed the area around their vehicle and home. They discovered that their newspaper had been torn up and thrown about, and some towels had been taken from a box on the side porch of the house.

The March 4, 2008, edition of *The Item* reported on the story under the headline "Return of the Lizard Man?" The paper noted that Dixie was concerned about a number of cats that they had on the property. As the paper reported:

"Rawson said about 20 cats typically sleep in their barn and by the side of their house. After the incident, about half the cats were missing and haven't returned.

"'I don't think they were hurt,' Dixie said, 'I think they are just terrified.'"

While the story harkened back to the 1988 mauling of the Wayes' vehicle, the culprit in the Rawson case seemed more likely to be known animals such as coyotes or wild dogs.

Coyotes had been reported in the area and it's possible they were after the Rawsons' cats who took refuge under and on the vehicle. But coyotes typically hunt in packs and such a fight would have produced a considerable amount of noise. One of the things that puzzled the Rawsons was why they hadn't been disturbed by the ruckus in the night.

Blood samples were collected from the van and sent to the State Law Enforcement Division for analysis. When the results came back later, the report stated that the "likely culprit" was a domestic dog.

The report didn't sit well with a lot of people and there were things about the case that made the domestic dog conclusion sound absurd. The van had taken over two thousand dollars' worth of damage and it was hard to believe that a common, domestic dog could have bitten and chewed the metal so extensively.

Liston Truesdale had already retired by the time the Rawsons' car was mauled, but Sheriff E.J. Melvin investigated the case. While waiting for the results of the blood test, Melvin decided to look around in the fields near the Rawsons' home to see if he could determine what was responsible for the damage. In a field not far from the van, the sheriff found two dead animals: a cow and a coyote.

WIS Channel 10 covered the story and referred to it as a "renewed investigation into the 'Lizard Man.'" The station noted:

"We have learned that two dead animals were found in a field near the home of Dixie and Bob Rawson. The Lee County Sheriff's Department says it could be linked to some pretty serious damage to the Rawsons' van."

The sheriff suggested it was further evidence that coyotes were responsible for the damage on the Rawsons' vehicle, but his bizarre find led people to ask—what had killed the coyote and the cow? It was yet another puzzling component of the strange events in Lee County.

Three years later, yet another car mauling occurred. On the morning of July 4, 2011, Leon and Ada Marshall discovered that their 2009 Dodge Journey had been damaged during the night. Like the previous cases, there were bite marks and damage to the fenders as well as the bumper. Bishopville's mysterious monster seemed to have a taste for Dodge vehicles.

Not much came of the Marshall incident. Although evidence of some kind of animal was found at the scene, the sheriff's office didn't send it for testing.

Every few years a Lizard Man story crops up in Lee County. Sometimes they're simple whispers of an odd sighting. Other times, they're more dramatic and, well, questionable.

Take the report from August 2015 when a woman leaving Sunday church service in Bishopville reportedly walked out to see the Lizard Man himself strolling along in front of a cluster of trees. The woman snapped a photo and immediately contacted a television station to report the incident.

"My hand to God, I am not making this up. So excited," the woman, identified only as "Sarah from Sumter," told Mt. Pleasant, SC's ABC News 4, WCIV-TV.

The photo, which can be viewed online with a quick search, is, well, absurd at best and shows a cartoonish-like character that many took to be a man in a costume. Whether or not "Sarah from Sumter" was in on the gag or was fooled by the sighting is anyone's guess.

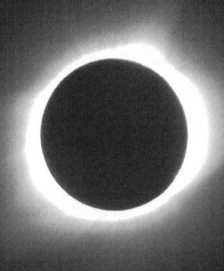

The Lizard's Legacy

Many of those who were a part of the Lizard Man saga are now gone. Chris Davis, the most famous witness, died tragically in 2009, murdered in a drug related incident in his own home. Davis was 37 years old and had never wavered from his story about the creature.

Liston Truesdale retired from the sheriff's department in 1992 and passed away in 2015. He is still remembered for his investigations into Bishopville's weird creature reports.

During the height of Lizardmania in 1988, Lizard Man products were a hot commodity in the area. T-shirts, hats, and other items depicting the reptilian swamp monster were being sold in countless shops and even at roadside stands.

While the furor has died down, the town of Bishopville hasn't forgotten its hometown cryptid. The South Carolina Cotton Museum in Bishopville has a Lizard Man display with items from the case, including one of the original track castings.

An annual Lizard Man festival is held each fall, and plenty of people still talk about the creature.

In 2017, an official warning regarding the cryptid was even issued by state authorities. The South Carolina Emergency Management Division tweeted about the upcoming solar eclipse and warned residents that the event might lead to a reemergence of the Lizard Man. People of Lee and Sumter counties were warned to "remain vigilant for sightings of Lizard Man."

The burning question remains, what exactly was (and maybe still is) roaming around Scape Ore Swamp?

Students of the strange have puzzled over the case and speculated on a wide range of possibilities. The mere idea of a two legged, walking reptile man may sound like the stuff of B-movies, but even some scientists have put serious thought into it.

Dale A. Russell, curator of vertebrate fossils at the National Museum of Canada in Ottawa, put forth a theory in 1982 that involved what he called a "Dinosauroid."

As John LeMay notes in *Southerners & Saurians: Swamp Monsters, Lizard Men and Other Curious Creatures of the Old South*:

"Russell proposed that a dinosaur called the Troodon could have evolved into something more akin to a human. His reasoning for this was that the Troodon had an encephalization quotient—or EQ—six times higher than normal dinosaurs. Or, in simpler terms, it had a bigger brain than other dinosaurs in its size class, meaning it had a higher capacity for intelligence.

"Russell believed that if the trend in Troodon evolution had continued to the present, its brain case could by now be comparable to that of a human's. Russell also pointed out that Troodontids had good use of the digits on their forelimbs for grasping and manipulation of objects. Notably, the Troodon had three fingers, just like the 1988 Lizard Man."

Russell, a palaeontologist, teamed up with artist and model-maker Ron Seguin to create a sculpture of the dinosauroid. It's a somewhat creepy image of exactly what it sounds like—a bipedal, reptilian humanoid, albeit, without a tail.

But could such a thing have developed? And if so, why would it be so active in Scape Ore Swamp?

While most people have a concept of the classical image of South Carolina's Lizard Man, complete with green scales and a long lizard tail, it's important to note that this image is not backed up by most witness accounts.

People were certainly reporting a large, bipedal creature, but the idea of a walking alligator seems to have been derived more from the name Lizard Man and assumptions of its appearance rather than actual account details.

Chris Davis never mentioned the creature having a tail, nor did witnesses like the Elmores or Blythers.

For all intents and purposes, it seems clear that most of the witnesses were seeing what we would define as a Sasquatch, or in Southern lingo, a Skunk Ape.

Skunk Ape reports have come from swamps all over the South, and it's believed they can thrive in such environments. It's easy to imagine a Skunk Ape strolling out of a place like the Scape Ore Swamp, covered in mud and slime from the swampy waters, and looking even more bizarre and unusual than it would even under normal conditions.

For that matter, perhaps caked and dried mud could give a witness the impression of scales.

Whatever the case, the mystery of the Bishopville Lizard Man has never been solved and remains to this day one of the Palmetto State's most curious monster tales.

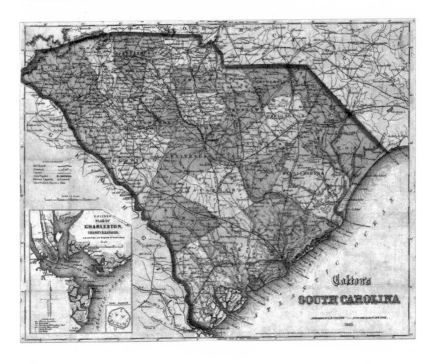

PALMETTO STATE MONSTERS by David Weatherly

PART THREE
Bigfoot in the Palmetto State

South Carolina Bigfoot

While South Carolina certainly doesn't rank near the top for Bigfoot sightings, there are still plenty of interesting accounts that indicate the creatures are present in the state.

Although South Carolina is smaller in size, it is nestled between two states with high numbers of Bigfoot accounts—Georgia and North Carolina, so it really should come as no surprise to expect the creatures in the Palmetto State, even if they may just be passing through.

Intriguingly, it's a state where the actual numbers of encounters may be much higher than they initially seem.

My colleague Mike Richburg grew up in South Carolina and has investigated sightings in the state for years. Most of the reports he follows up on are ones that he personally collects, and as a result, they don't end up on the radar of any of the large Bigfoot researcher organizations.

Mike Richburg's years of personal research have led him to conclude that there are two different kinds of hairy bipeds in South Carolina.

The first is typically described as at least seven feet in height with reddish brown hair and human-like features. Reports of these creatures are mostly found in the Pee Dee region of the state.

The second type of creature, Richburg says, is always reported as being under seven feet in height and resembles gorillas more than humans, with thick black hair and bulky bodies. Reports of these types of creatures typically come from the state's Lowcountry and coast region, especially near the Wateree, Congaree, and Santee Rivers.

Of course, these two variations could be the same type of

creature that has developed differently over time as it adapted to its environment.

One thing is clear, South Carolina is a state that bears a closer look in terms of its Sasquatch activity, and it will be interesting to see what researchers continue to find in the state's wild regions.

Congaree National Park.

Early Accounts

One of the most interesting, historic Bigfoot accounts to come out of South Carolina involves a native American hunting party and its run-in with a large, hairy beast in the summer of 1889.

The story was reported in July of that year and made the rounds in several papers, as was the custom of the time. The original report was published by the *Advertiser* out of Clarksville, Georgia. According to the paper, a hunting party had established a camp east of the Tugalo River in what is now Oconee County, South Carolina. The party went out for a day of hunting and left a deer they had killed the evening before at their camp. When they returned from the day's hunt, they discovered the deer was gone. The following day, the same thing occurred. When it was time for the next day's hunt, the men left one of their own behind to watch over the camp. An older man was selected to guard things that day, and when the intruder returned to the camp, the man received quite a shock. A monster came and took the deer carcass.

The guard said the beast was seven feet tall, hairy all over, and walked on two legs like a man. He added that the thing's "mouth was in the chin" and that it had large claws on both its fingers and toes. The man was too shocked, or too afraid, to fire at the creature.

One can only imagine the reaction of his comrades when the man related his tale. The following day, all seven hunters decided to remain in camp with the deer they had killed. Sure enough, the beast returned. According to the report in the *Advertiser*:

"The monster came, gathered up the deer and started off, when one of them fired at it, the ball taking effect in the back.

The animal dropped the deer and turned and started toward them, when the other six poured a volley into its breast and it fell dead."

Three hours later, the men started hearing a noise that they estimated was about a mile away. "Yahoo, yahoo, yahoo!" someone, or something, was shouting. The men quickly left the camp and soon called on a posse to pursue what they believed was another creature.

A party took off on horseback with hunting dogs along to track the beast. According to the paper, the men finally located the thing:

"When the men appeared in sight, the animal would run, but it could whip every dog they could get after it. The party pursued it to the river and at jumps it went across over into Habersham County and was shot by a party soon after it crossed the river."

Unfortunately, the intriguing account ends there. There seems to be no follow up to the tale, and, as is often the case with accounts of the period, we're left to wonder about the veracity of the account.

Several sources, including Rick Berry's *Bigfoot on the East Coast*, mention accounts of a large hairy creature around the turn of the century in the Black River area. The beast reportedly harassed residents in the region enough that it gained a local nickname—"Red Eye." The monster was described as being a large, man-like beast covered in hair, presumably with red eyes.

In his book *Strange South Carolina*, Sherman Carmichael mentions stories involving a purported wild woman in Outland, in Williamsburg County. Unfortunately, there are no dates associated with the accounts, nor are there any witness names or specific locations provided, making it difficult to search for any further information or potential accounts. Carmichael notes that the tales have been handed down orally.

The wild woman was spotted the first time by a tobacco farmer out on his morning routine of driving workers to the fields in his pickup truck. While the farmer himself didn't see the figure the first time, his son and several of the farmhands he was transporting did. The strange entity darted across the road and vanished into the nearby woods.

The farmer and his son investigated and discovered what looked like the tracks of a woman. They followed for a short distance, but soon lost the trail due to pine needles and thick ground cover.

The farmer attempted to find the trail later that day with hunting dogs in tow, but the animals refused to go very deep into the woods.

In short order, there was another sighting of the creature. A woman a mile from the tobacco farm went outside one evening to burn her trash. She discovered debris thrown around the yard. She typically used a wire cage to burn the refuse in order to prevent animals from digging in it. When she rounded the corner of her home, she found the source of the disturbance. As Carmichael reports:

"She saw a strange figure digging in the garbage. The creature resembled a human female with hair that hung to the ground. The woman ran back into the house and waited for the arrival of her husband. When her husband arrived, the creature was gone. The description of the mysterious woman and the tracks resembled those of the first sighting."

The sightings reportedly stopped for a time until the wild woman showed up again in upper Georgetown County. This time, a man out checking his cows found one of them mutilated near the woods. Scanning the area for wild animals, the man spotted an "ape woman eating a piece of raw meat."

Once she realized the man had seen her, she headed into the woods and disappeared.

Carmichael also briefly mentions another sighting in the Pine Bluff area near the Big Pee Dee River. The report states that the wild woman was heading into Carvers Bay.

The town of Easley had a "gorilla scare" in the summer of 1925. According to an article in Greenville, South Carolina's *News* dated July 31, Easley had suffered an "epidemic of gorillaitis" that had lasted several days. The article asserts that those with weak hearts were suffering in stark terror and people were hiding inside their homes for fear of running into the creature. Of course, the situation was quickly blamed on a traveling carnival.

According to the paper:

"Some weeks ago, a carnival company visited Central, the prosperous little community along the main line of the Southern just west of Easley. It was reported that a large and ferocious gorilla escaped from the show company while doing its stuff at Central. Terror spread through all the land round about."

The town of Easley had a gorilla scare in 1925.

A few days after the purported escape, a gorilla was allegedly spotted around Easley. In short order, tracks were found. Pieces of dead chickens were discovered in neighborhood yards, fences were torn down, cats became scarce, and dogs started hiding under houses howling all night. The paper reported that people in the area had reached their limit:

"The situation became unbearable and the other day men, a large crowd of them—an Easley citizen says 40 of them—shouldered their guns and took to the open about Easley to find the gorilla which had been eating chickens, chasing vagrant canines under houses, and otherwise playing the very heck. They trailed and trailed and found pieces of dead chickens, broken fences, downtrodden peach trees, and other signs and indications of depredation."

Despite the posse's efforts, no gorilla was found and in short order, the truth was revealed when the "gorilla's brother" came forward.

The story claims that an area man heard about the escaped gorilla and decided to have a bit of fun with the townsfolk. He cut out wooden impressions of gigantic gorilla feet, including clear cuts for the toes. He added rubber pieces to the heels, nailed the wooden feet to his own shoes, and proceeded to tromp around town at night, throwing chicken feathers about and tearing down fences.

According to the news report, the culprit's name had not been made officially public and the townspeople were scared but enjoyed the laugh.

The story is curious in several ways. Was the news report itself a hoax, or was it really a report about a hoaxed monster?

It seems odd that the townsfolk would "have a laugh" after fences were torn up and a posse spent hours of their time tracking a creature that had terrified residents only to find out it was all a prank. Whatever the case, the Easley gorilla scare came and went quickly.

A creature lurking around Rock Hill in early 1938 got a bit more attention. A UP (United Press) story dated February 5 dubbed the beast "The Monster of Marmotte Street" and linked it to sightings in Mobile, Alabama. The news item posited that the creature had made its way to Rock Hill where it was dubbed the "African Udilacus" by locals.

Coincidentally, police officials in Mobile had investigated the creature sightings there for a week but stated that they believed the beast had finally run off into the swamp and vanished.

Naturally, there was a quick assumption that the creature had escaped from a circus that was wintering in the area, but officials confirmed that the troupe had lost no animals.

Rock Hill's African Udilacus was first reported near a cotton mill section on the outskirts of town. Area resident John White spotted the beast and reported:

"It was standing in the water. It was black and tall as a man. I threw a rock at it, but it snarled and started after me. I ran."

Bruce Neal was with White at the time, and he said the monster had a foul odor and that "After it chased us a little ways, it dropped down on all fours."

According to other witness accounts, the thing was fierce, fur covered, and resembled a gorilla. One man claimed the creature attacked him and ripped some of his clothing from his body before he managed to escape its clutches.

Columbus, Nebraska's *Telegram* reported on the monster in its February 7, 1938, edition, noting that people around Rock Hill were carrying clubs as protection against the creature. According to the *Telegram* the shambling thing had long hair. The paper also reported that the monster had killed two dogs and mauled "not less than a dozen" others.

Sam Watts reported that he was chased through the woods by a hairy creature that was making grunting sounds, and other, similar reports came in about the nocturnal monster.

Constable Carl Hovis reported that he took two shots at some kind of "shambling beast" and believed it was the same thing that residents were reporting.

By February 9, the creature had reportedly moved on from Rock Hill. A report in that day's edition of the *Southwest Times* out of Pulaski, Virginia, announced: "African Udilacus Departs Carolina After Wild Spree."

Speculation about why the creature disappeared ranged from thoughts that it had returned to Alabama to a rumor that it had gone into hibernation for ten years and would return in the next decade.

The *Times* couldn't resist throwing out the circus animal idea once again, but this time with a slight twist, noting:

"Authorities who investigated the mystery said the "thing" may have been one of the [hamadryad] or sacred baboons being trained by Tommy Burns at York, South Carolina. Burns, a circus animal trainer, said he did not believe any of his animals were loose but sometimes the monkeys got out and ran free."

Whatever the case, Rock Hill's African Udilacus was gone and there were no reports of it returning on the ten-year anniversary of the sightings.

Early Accounts

Bigfoot Through the Decades

1960s

A BFRO report details a Hampton County incident from June 15, 1964. The reporting witness submitted details about an encounter his brother had near the Salkehatchie River between Estill and Hampton. As the report states:

"My brother, Doug S, was out camping with friends one Friday night. It was late, my grandmother and I were watching TV. Doug suddenly burst into the house, scared and wild-eyed. "Bigfoot! Bigfoot!" he came in yelling. "Bigfoot ran us off!" Doug was always very brave, and I had never seen him scared like that in my life. He had a shotgun with him, but he said he didn't shoot it because he was afraid it would kill him if he did, so he ran."

The boy told his family that the group had a campfire going when they suddenly heard a lot of noise around them. A "tall, hairy, man-like creature appeared," terrifying the campers and sending them fleeing.

Doug and his brother returned to the campsite the following day to retrieve the gear that was left behind. While there, Doug acted nervous and frightened, watching the woods carefully lest the creature make another appearance.

The camp itself had been ransacked and items were scattered all over. The campfire had been scattered as well and there were strange footprints around the area. The boys gathered up what they could and left the area quickly. The reporting witness was very affected by his brother's behavior, noting:

"Doug and I had been stalked by wild cats in the swamp before, faced and killed wild boars and had to kill huge snakes.

We had all kinds of adventures in the swamps and woods as kids, but I had never seen him scared, much less terrified, before."

The story got around the area fast and the boys tried to talk to their grandfather about the beast, but they were met with ridicule.

A week later, another story circulated in the area. A truck driver with a national transport line came into Hampton and wanted to speak with police officers about an encounter he'd had with a Bigfoot.

"He had left Savannah in his 18-wheeler and was on his way to Charleston. He saw a Bigfoot in the road and had to either stop or hit the creature. He stopped and the Bigfoot either banged on the door or jumped onto the hood. The truck driver was terrified and fled the scene."

Reportedly, the truck driver's story was reported in the *Hampton County Guardian*, though I have been unable to locate the original article.

A soldier from Fort Jackson had a frightening encounter in the Congaree in 1964.

A soldier from Fort Jackson on a training mission in the Congaree Swamp in the fall of 1964 had a frightening experience. The man was alone and was taking part in an escape and evasion exercise.

Not long after dark, around seven p.m., the man was walking down a dirt fire lane road when he heard something approaching him. It was a moonless night so visibility was poor, but he could tell that whatever was coming was bipedal. He assumed it was a person, so he stopped walking and waited in his position. When the figure sounded close, the soldier called out, asking, "Who goes there?"

He estimated that the figure went about fifty to seventy-five feet away and stopped. Still expecting a human response, the man was puzzled by what occurred next. "I heard what sounded like someone talking backwards in a sort of growl as I was standing there confused about what was going on."

After a moment, whatever it was started walking toward the man again. The soldier knelt down on one knee and remained very still. He waited until the figure came out of the trees, then he stood up quickly and said, "I got you!"

"That's when all hell broke loose," the man reports. Whatever the thing was, it took off in a mad run, "crashing through the brush like a train."

The soldier was thoroughly shaken up at this point and began to run himself. He headed down the fire lane in the pitch dark and ran for a good distance before stopping. He stood and listened to see if there were any sounds of pursuit from whatever he had encountered.

Despite being a trained soldier and experienced hunter and outdoorsman, the man was terrified. Even though there was no indication that the thing was following him, he continued running and eventually came upon a sergeant who was waiting at the extraction point.

"I never wanted to see a person so badly before," the man states. Whatever was lurking in the swamp that night, it left a lasting impression on the soldier.

Ray Crowe's *Bigfoot Behavior Volume II* lists a brief note about a spring 1966 sighting reported by a woman and her husband.

The couple were at South Pier in Beaufort when they spotted something moving behind a rock. It was nighttime but the creature was illuminated by the moonlight as it came out. According to the report, the thing was a "hunched-over ape." The beast moved towards the couple with its arms swinging. The husband turned on the vehicle's headlights and the sudden brightness sent the thing running for the woods. The witnesses stated that the creature moved faster than any human.

1970s

A witness reported to the BFRO that she'd had a number of Bigfoot related experiences growing up in the community of Lincolnville near Summerville in Charleston County in 1970.

She reported the incidents in 2006 when she was 47 years of age but recalled the experiences vividly.

The first notable incident was in June 1970 while she was playing outside with other children. The group noticed an overpowering smell. The property she lived on was between one and two acres and had chain link fencing. In the woods behind the fence, the witness saw glowing red eyes peering at the group. She reports that the height was taller than a man, but she did not see any other details.

On several occasions, the same powerful, foul smell was noticed around the property. During this period, a number of dogs in the area were killed by something that crushed their skulls.

The witness also reports camping out with a friend in an old mobile home on the back of the property one night when something circled around outside. The creature walked around the trailer, pounding on the sides. The girls believed the thing was trying to enter the home.

On another occasion, the witness heard the same sound hitting the sides of her house. The girl's brother was frightened and said that the creature had appeared at his window. When family members rushed outside, they heard something large walking off into the woods and away from the property.

The most significant incident came in October 1970 when the witness got a good look at the Bigfoot. The girl had gone outside to tend to the pumphouse when she spotted the thing, as she reports:

"I saw, in the early morning sunshine, this creature that looked like an ape standing on the other side of the fence watching me. It was tall, had dark brown hair, and it had a sloping forehead that looked like some kind of ape. I could not see the eyes because they were hooded. It was standing there just kind of rocking side to side.

Rick Berry writes that in early 1970, a couple was sitting in a vehicle at Black Creek when a large, bipedal hairy creature reached in through a window and grabbed the man by his shirt. The man was so shocked that he reportedly passed out. This may have surprised the creature, since, according to the female witness, the thing quickly ran away.

Berry also mentions a brief anecdote from a man named Nemo Frye from December 1970. According to Frye, pilots from the US Marine Corps Air Station in Beaufort had reported seeing large, gorilla-like creatures roaming around some of the uninhabited islands on the flight path to their runway.

Frye himself mentions going hunting on Old Island with a group of friends the same month. Reportedly, the party's hunting dogs all refused to get out of the boat. The canines huddled together in a corner in fright and could not be convinced to move.

Berry also mentions an incident from Pritchards Island where a woman reportedly saw a large, hairy man-like creature in the water. The beast appeared to be playing like a child would. No further details were provided.

An Air Force security police officer on the Air Force Base at Myrtle Beach saw a Sasquatch on April 18, 1974. According to the man's report to the BFRO, he was patrolling Serpentine Road around nine o'clock at night when the incident occurred.

The moon was full, and the officer had turned the lights of his vehicle off to see if he could navigate using only the moonlight. The area is restricted, and the patrolman didn't expect to see anyone. As he rounded a curve in the road, he turned his headlights back on and was shocked to see a figure that was in mid-stride about to leap across a ditch on the roadside. As the man watched, the creature jumped with ease and vanished into the trees in a matter of seconds.

The witness reports that the beast was covered in "light brown fur." He further notes:

"The creature stood about 7-8 feet tall and probably weighed about 400 to 450 lbs. For its size and obvious weight, it had remarkable agility and speed. The jump that it made cleared 14 to 16 feet with no problem. It had a body like a large human covered with hair.

"I called my flight chief and had him meet me out on the Serpentine Road where I explained to him what I saw as was my duty at the time. He said that he believed me but thought it was in the best interest of my career to not put this report on the police blotter that night and that I should simply forget about the incident altogether. Until now, I have done just that."

Florida's *St. Petersburg Times* ran a report on potential Bigfoot activity in South Carolina in its July 8, 1974, edition. Reporter Red Marston chronicled the incident that had occurred several years before involving a group of hunters.

The story involved a former Clearwater, Florida, radio announcer named Dean Poucher. Poucher had grown up in the Seminole-Clearwater area of Florida. After moving to South Carolina, Poucher found strange tracks on two different occasions.

Poucher said the first incident took place when he was part of a group of five hunters who had gone to an unnamed island to hunt. According to Poucher:

"We had gained special permission from the owner who warned us that the interior was so thick it would be impossible to penetrate, not even by trained Marines from Camp LeJeune. We had been informed that the year previous some other hunters went to the island and certainly did find the interior impassable. But that hunting trip was really spoiled because the dogs absolutely refused to hunt.

"Well, on our trip, we had two boats and two of the finest dogs in all Beaufort County. We landed on a narrow, sandy beach and gathered to lay out our battle strategy."

As soon as they were on the island, the men, all experienced hunters, spotted signs of game. They were eager to set off but soon ran into a complication. As Poucher notes:

"We proceeded to implement the game plan and it was then we noticed the strange behavior of our dogs. They wouldn't get out of the boat they were in. They sat shivering miserably with their tails between their legs. The owner, who had been popping off about his great deer dogs, was both embarrassed and mad. He finally dragged them out by the collar, hauled them up the beach to the tree line, and jammed their noses into fresh deer tracks. Then he turned them loose, but the dogs turned tail and ran back to the boat. Both leaped in there and sat there shivering."

Not knowing what to make of the hunting dogs' reactions, the hunters set off anyway without the animals. When they entered the woods, they didn't encounter any game, but both Poucher and another man saw something unusual. Both men kept the incidents to themselves until they met later.

A chance meeting a few days after the hunt gave the men the opportunity to speak. It turned out that they had both found odd tracks at opposite ends of the island. Poucher says the tracks he saw were buried in a foot of blue marsh mud, but the size and the needed weight to make the impressions was unforgettable.

"I will never forget their size, nor the depth to which they were sunk. My boot alongside, a size 11, was hardly half as large as the track. To compare, I put my full weight on one boot, but I sank less than an inch into the mud. My guess is that our big-footed friend would tip the scales at three to four times my weight, placing him somewhere between 600 and 800 pounds."

Poucher's friend reported tracks that were eighteen inches long and between seven and nine inches wide with no instep. The man came to the same conclusions as Poucher in terms of the creature's likely weight.

Three years later Poucher was in the same region, this time walking with his wife Ann along a dock on a different, uninhabited island. They had a view of the island that Poucher had previously spotted the giant tracks on. Poucher recounts:

"I happened to look down at the mud bank alongside the dock. It was low tide. There were the tracks! They came up out of the creek and disappeared into the thickness of the island."

It's important to note that Poucher was a former executive secretary of the Beaufort Chamber of Commerce, and not one prone to fabricate stories. Some would say that he was lucky to have found such tracks not once, but twice, though he decided to leave well enough alone and not try to find the creature on either occasion.

In July 1975, a young man in Oconee County had a strange encounter in a remote forested area at Lake Keowee.

It was twilight and the fifteen-year-old boy was out for a

walk when he saw a large figure moving up an incline across a dirt road. The thing was headed into dense forest. The witness reported:

"I was approximately 50 yards away when it saw me. The light was very low, but I saw this thing was not human at all, at least 7 to 8 ft. tall, 450 lbs., no neck and reddish in color."

Panicked, the boy fled the scene as quickly as he could. As he was running, he heard a sound he describes as a "horrible scream like a cow and pig being killed on a loudspeaker."

The witness also heard loud foot falls crashing through the brush behind him. He reported the incident to the BFRO in 2009 and researcher Don Tart followed up on the account. Tart said he spoke with the witness several times and found him believable.

The witness also noted that there were other stories in the area of people seeing the creature, and Tart himself notes that there continue to be reports from both sides of the lake.

The investigator also reports that just north of the sighting area is a road named "Screaming Hollow," and across the lake another road known as "Booger Branch." Both names are a further indication of the body of folklore in the area associated with Bigfoot.

The Bigfoot Encounters website has an article with several Bigfoot accounts submitted by a writer listed only as "mpmjr."

The first account comes from the writer's sister and took place in 1977 or 1978 around the bottom of Henry's Knob Mountain in the town of Clover. The girl and a companion were sitting in a parked car late one night when a large, hairy creature picked up the back of the vehicle and started pushing. According to the account, the driver could not get control of the car because it was being moved about so hard. The couple did manage to escape, although further details are not provided. When the girl arrived home, she reported the incident to family members, stating that the bipedal creature the couple encountered was about nine feet tall.

Another of the writer's sisters also had a Bigfoot encounter in the same area. They were inside a mobile home at the time. As the report states:

"One night she and my sister said they heard very heavy breathing as if the trailer itself was breathing. That following morning, my brother-in-law walked around the trailer and found one huge footprint in the ground."

Apparently, the writer's family are magnets for creature sightings since, according to the article, mpmjr's niece also had a sighting. No date is listed but the incident occurred when the girl was young and in the same area as the writer's other listed sightings. According to the girl, she had seen a large, hairy creature in the woods around her home. Gruesomely, she claims to have observed the beast biting the head off a cat.

In early 1977, a creature was reportedly running around Fort Mill in York County. Fort Mill is close to the North Carolina border and is considered a suburb of Charlotte, NC.

The February 14 headline in the *Rock Hill Evening Herald* begged the question: "Bigfoot—Is Print a Prank or Genuine?"

The article went on to recount:

"The cops call it a prank. But the people who found it in their back yard don't think it's so funny. Somebody or something's been barefootin' in their vegetable patch. Whoever or whatever it was left one big-toed, flat-footed, bare muddy print between the dried-up bell pepper plants and the frozen tomato stalks."

Helen Gromoske told reporters that she and her husband first thought the track was that of a bear, but there were no claws visible. The track was first discovered by Helen's thirteen-year-old grandson, Leonard. The boy was playing football with a friend when their ball landed in the garden. Going to retrieve it, the boys spotted the footprint and rushed in to report it.

Helen Gromoske brushed the boy's statement off at first, but finally she and her husband went out to investigate. They were stunned at the find and covered the print with a washtub to protect it from rain.

Sadly, the Fort Mill police department didn't take the report seriously. One officer stated that he wanted to know if anyone had spotted King Kong in the area.

The head of the South Carolina Game Commission had an explanation for the anomalous print. He told reporters that the print "Could have been created by an air pocket in the ground created when the ground was frozen. With nice weather, the ground thawed, and dirt fell in where the air pocket was."

It's surprising the Commissioner didn't blame the track on swamp gas or a one-legged escaped circus animal.

The *Rock Hill Herald* followed up with another report the following day, confirming that Fort Mill Police Chief Floyd Foss believed the print was a fake.

Mrs. Gromoske was by now rather disturbed at the whole incident, stating: "It gives you an eerie feeling, knowing that something could be that close. It makes you feel uneasy."

Ray Liguori, curator of the York County Nature Museum, was more interested in the print and made a plaster cast of it. Liguori said he was puzzled by the print and even more so by the fact that there was only a single one in evidence. "It's not a human foot, I'll tell you that," Liguori stated.

The print measured over twelve inches long and was comparable in size to a man's size fourteen shoe. "An animal with a foot that size would have to weigh 400 pounds, and it would make a deeper indication than that," the curator stated.

The Gromoske family received a number of phone calls after reporting the print, and random people started showing up on the property, mostly curiosity seekers intrigued by the monster track. Helen Gromoske said she had felt it her duty to report the find but wasn't impressed by the attention the family received. "If there is a danger, I would want my child protected. I just wish it had been in somebody else's yard," she said.

Not long after the print find at the Gromoske property, another incident was reported 75 miles away in Saluda County west of Columbia. This time, there were numerous footprints, in fact, there were hundreds.

D.W. Berry, who owned the farm where the tracks were discovered, wasn't sure what to make of them but said they looked real to him. According to a report in the February 20 edition of Charleston's *News and Courier*, the tracks were discovered by Berry's grandson and another boy. The tracks were on what the family referred to as the "Old Homestead," about ten miles from Saluda.

"They were setting some traps down there when they heard a noise. They said it was a terrible sound, like a bobcat. They were really shook up right after it happened," Berry reported. The boys quickly left the area after the strange sound. Soon after, large flat-footed tracks were found on the property.

The prints that were found measured fourteen inches in length and seven inches in width. The stride was unusually long—four feet—a further indication that whatever had made the tracks was very large in size.

Reportedly, screams like the ones reported by the boys had been heard in the area for years, though no one offered an explanation for the sounds.

According to some sources, law enforcement took the case more seriously than their cohorts in Fort Mill had taken the Gromoske incident because, this time, several cows had been killed in the county and the deaths were considered mysterious. But at least one official, Saluda County Sheriff Department's David P. Charles, believed the whole thing was a sham, stating: "It's more of a joke than anything else. I think it's a hoax."

When the path of the tracks was traced, it was discovered that they wound through briars and brambles, circled a pond, went down a little used road and over a sawdust pile to a creek bank and pasture before circling back around to the pond. No further evidence of the track maker was found.

Like the Gromoske family, Berry said that word of the find on his property drew in a lot of people who wanted to see the monster tracks. He estimated that around three hundred people had shown up to see the prints for themselves.

A woman submitted a report to the BFRO detailing her memories of a Bigfoot sighting that she'd had when she was a child in the summer of 1978 in Barnwell County.

She was playing with her brother and a neighbor on a country road near some old railroad tracks one evening when they heard a high-pitched screeching or wailing sound. They went toward the old tracks to investigate and were shocked to see a large creature on the other side of the tracks.

She describes the beast as being at least seven feet tall with long arms and long tufts of dark brown hair that covered its body. The creature was just as surprised to see the children as they were to see it.

The woman says the sighting lasted about fifteen seconds and that she turned and ran for her house, screaming all the way. Her brother and friend joined her in the retreat. She added further details about the creature:

"As best as I can recall, its face was oddly human-like in appearance yet at the same time seemed like an ape. It did not make any noise at all once we all saw each other. It just stood there looking at us but seemed to be peaceful and it certainly appeared not to be hostile. Its sheer size is what scared me so badly."

The area of the sighting is close to the Salkehatchie River and there are numerous creeks and tributaries in the region, making it an area rich in resources.

The witness and her brother avoided talking about the incident for years, but when they finally did, their memories of the encounter and the creature matched.

One especially intense account of a Bigfoot comes from South Carolina investigator Mike Richburg and was, in large part, his impetus for becoming a cryptid researcher in his adult years.

Well before sunrise on a fall day in 1978, then fourteen-year-old Richburg set out to go hunting with his father. The pair traveled southeast of Columbia where they met up with a group of other deer hunters for a group hunt at a place with the ominous name of the Devil's Orchard Swamp. The area is along the Congaree River and is rich with game. The men planned to use hunting dogs to flush deer out and send them in the direction of some of the hunters who would wait in position along one side of the river.

The mysterious Congaree.

The group met for breakfast at a local diner, then headed out to the swamp for the hunt. According to the group's game plan, Mike and his father would take up positions along the southernmost point along the Congaree, so they were the last two to be dropped off. The sun was just starting to come up as the pair trekked off on foot into the woods.

When they got close to the river, Mike's father directed him to head down the bank and find a good spot to wait until the deer came their way. Mike started walking as his father headed off in the opposite direction upstream. Mike jumped over a small stream, then worked his way through thick trees, treading carefully through patches of fog. The young man was close to where the riverbank overhung the water when he found a spot to sit on the edge of a small clearing. He settled down to wait and listened to the sounds of morning breaking in the wild.

Richburg had only been sitting in his position for a few minutes when he heard something that caught his attention. It sounded like something large coming up out of the water and climbing the riverbank. He quickly shouldered his shotgun and took the safety off, expecting to see a deer come up from the water. Instead, he saw something that he wasn't at all prepared for.

As the animal got closer, Mike started having the uneasy feeling that it wasn't a deer at all but something else. The way the creature moved around in the brush caused the young man to start thinking he was dealing with something much larger than a deer. "I got to thinking it was a big hog or something, which wouldn't be good since I had a little ol' 20 guage," Mike recalls.

The young hunter remained still, waiting for a clear look at the animal. If it was a large hog, he was hoping that it would ignore him and take off in another direction. But the situation became more unnerving when the creature made a sound. "The best way I can describe it is like a sigh or grunt...a very human-like sound," Richburg says.

The strange sound sent a whole range of possibilities rushing through the teenager's mind. Perhaps it was a person in the brush, maybe an escaped convict or bank robber, Mike thought. For a teenager out alone in the woods, it was a frightening thought, but things were about to get much more disturbing when the identity of what was nearby was revealed.

As Richburg watched, the figure stepped out about forty feet from his position. Although its back was to him, Mike knew that it was not a person or ordinary animal. The creature was covered in black hair like that of a bear, but Mike was sure it was not a bear.

The thing stood on two legs like a man and was around seven feet tall. Its arms and shoulders were large and muscular. It was dripping wet from having climbed out of the water.

Mike tried to process what he was seeing, and the possibilities rushed through his mind. He knew it wasn't a bear, and while it looked somewhat like a gorilla, he knew it wasn't a gorilla either. It looked very human-like but it was certainly not a man.

Mike recalls how scared he was at the sight, noting how huge the creature was. He watched as the thing walked over to the spot where he had entered the clearing himself earlier. The creature then stopped and turned its head to the left and Mike suddenly realized the thing had probably picked up his scent. It stood still a few moments then moved off into the trees, pushing branches aside with its hands as a human would do.

Richburg let out the breath he had been holding and he started to shake. In seconds, the creature was deep in the trees and no longer visible. Mike listened as the sound of the thing's trek through the woods faded away.

The young hunter was suddenly overwhelmed from the experience. Tears ran down his face and he was still shaking from the encounter. He slowly composed himself. He flipped the shotgun's safety back on and took off running for the two-rut road where he and his father had been dropped off by the other hunters. Once there, he waited for his father to return. When the elder Richburg came back, he knew his son was upset about something, but the teenager simply said he wasn't feeling good. He just couldn't tell his father what he had seen in the woods. Fear of ridicule from his father and the other hunters caused him to keep his mouth shut about the incident but it was an experience that would ultimately change the course of his life and set him on a path to becoming a cryptid researcher and investigator.

1980s

Ray Crowe mentions a 1983 Bigfoot sighting in his *Bigfoot Behavior Volume III*. According to the account, a man named Cal was motorboating with his father on the Great Pee Dee River early one afternoon in 1983 or 1984 when the incident occurred. As Crowe reports:

"A hundred feet away they saw a reddish-brown Bigfoot squatting on the bank. It looked up and in a split second, dove into the water and was gone. 'We never did see it surface.'"

The report was also covered in *Weird Carolinas* and further details were added. Reportedly, Cal was shooting a .22 pistol when he noticed something to his left along the riverbank. Cal's cousin was also in the boat during the incident.

Cal stated that the creature was about the size of a large man and was covered in long, reddish-brown hair. Cal and the creature locked eyes before it quickly dove into the water. When the thing entered the water, it dove like a man, extending its arms forward like a diver would.

Cal and his father went to the spot where the Bigfoot had been crouched and inspected the area. All they found were smear marks in the clay on the riverbank. Cal's father hadn't seen the creature, but he did catch a glimpse of something large going into the water and the resulting splash it created.

Rick Berry listed an interesting 1986 encounter in *Bigfoot on the East Coast*. The secondhand report involved a man's grandfather who heard loud noises outside along with his pigs squealing in alarm. He went to investigate and spotted a "large hairy man-like creature running with two hogs, one under each arm."

The incident occurred at the "151 Bypass of Willis Drive" but no further location details were provided.

An account from September 1986 is listed by several sources, including the BFRO. The incident involved a teenager who was biking in a remote area of York County. The youth's dog was along for the trek and noticed the creature first. The thing was in a hollow, eating grapes when the biker spotted it. According to the account, the beast was "as tall as a small shed and was very large. It was covered with light brown hair. The face was very much like a Mongoloid man."

The witness also reported that the creature's teeth were yellowish. The dog turned and ran back toward home. While the witness watched, the creature moved toward him. Frightened, the biker followed the dog and headed quickly for home. Glancing back, he spotted the Bigfoot as it lumbered over a fence.

The BFRO has a report that details a July 1987 sighting from Oconee County near the town of Seneca.

The witness says that at the time of the sighting, there had been rumors of Bigfoot in the area for years. The reporting witness had assumed that the stories were designed to keep people out of the woods due to illegal plants being grown but notes that the story had also been told by an elderly woman who was a local minister, lending more credibility to the stories.

The sighting occurred between 7:45 and 8:30 in the morning along a route that the witness was very familiar with. As the report states:

"My sister and I were going to visit our friends. She was driving. We travel this route all the time...as we approached the small bridge that crosses a pond that we call a swamp, we both noticed it in the middle of the road. At first, I thought it was a bear. As she slowed the car and hit the horn, it stood up, looked in our direction, and took off across the swamp."

The witness stressed that having seen many bears in the area previously, she knew the creature on the road that day was definitely not a bear. When the creature ran away, it did so on four legs. The thing was large, covered with hair, and had no neck. It was dark brown and stood six to seven feet tall.

The witness believes the creature was eating roadkill that was at the spot.

A South Carolina resident sent me information about a Bigfoot that showed up in 1989 in Cold Point in Laurens County. The first report came in April from fifty-seven-year-old Martha Tollison. Tollison was driving to work at 5:30 in the morning when she spotted a "grayish-black giant" on the side of Indian Mound Road. She told a reporter from the *Spartanburg Herald*:

"I slowed down at first, but when I saw how big and tall it was, I took off. I just went by and it just kind of turned and went back in the woods."

Tollison's husband and family didn't take her sighting seriously, but they soon learned that she wasn't the only one in the area who had spotted the creature. According to the newspaper, at least nine people had spotted the thing along area roads.

Arlene McCall was among the witnesses who saw the creature. Like Tollison, McCall saw the beast on Indian Mound Road. She told reporters that the Bigfoot lingered on the side of the road for a few moments, then walked off into the trees on two legs.

Curiosity seekers and monster hunters searched the area, but no evidence of the creature was discovered, leaving many to wonder what the "Cold Point Creature" actually was.

Unfortunately, my contact was not able to provide the date of the original article and there were no further details of the beast available.

1990s

In *Bigfoot Across America*, Philip Rife listed an account of a road sighting that was originally posted online.

A couple driving in Dorchester County near Pineville in 1993 spotted a creature on the road. The man, who was driving at the time, described the incident:

"This thing stepped out in front of us. I hit the brakes. All I saw at first was two long, hairy legs. I started backing up so my lights would spot it better.

"This was no bear. This thing was maybe 7 or 8 feet tall and big, hairy, and wet. It didn't stand real straight, but more at a slump from the waist up. It had the reddest eyes I have ever seen, and it just looked at us. Frozen, looking, not moving at all. Just standing there.

"Then, it just looked to its left and leaned as his leg started to turn, then the other, taking about a three-foot stride until it was out of sight, gone into the woods. This thing walked on two feet and was not a bear."

A family in a rural area of Spartanburg County was terrified by the creature they saw one night in the summer of 1993. The reporting witness told the BFRO that the incident occurred on August 15 in the town of Inman. The family's small dog had been barking for an extended period and the witness finally went to see what had the animal so worked up. As the report states:

"There was this large, hairy animal crouched down in the gully which I thought was a large chow dog, so I stomped my foot and yelled at it to go away. When I did, it stood up like a human on two feet. It had light gray hair...6ft tall, it had large gorilla shoulders and no neck, a flat face."

According to the witness, the creature took a long time to turn around and moved in very slow motion. Then, it suddenly started running deeper into the woods, knocking down trees in the process.

The following day, the witness went back into the woods and discovered large footprints along with piles of squash that had large bite marks out of them. The witness believed the squash came from a neighbor's garden.

The reporting witness added that numerous people in the area had seen black and brown Bigfoot creatures near the swamps and that a cave in the swamp was reportedly a hot spot where hunters reported seeing the creatures and hearing them scream.

A couple driving through Sumter County in August 1995

spotted what may have been a juvenile Bigfoot while driving close to Shaw Air Force Base. As the man told the BFRO:

"My wife and I saw a small, childlike Bigfoot while in South Carolina....it crossed the road in front of us, about 25 yards ahead of the car. It stopped in the middle of the road and looked at us, then it jumped to the other side into a swamp and was gone."

The witness said the creature was around five foot tall and had long hair on its arms, legs, and face. It was dark brown in color and proportionate in size to a ten or eleven-year-old boy.

The man reported that the sighting was around 1:30 a.m. at a little bridge a few miles east of Sumter. He adds that the creature's movements were very unusual: "One striking thing about it is the walking gait it had. Not like a man and not like a monkey. It would be very hard to imitate such a walk."

The December 1994 issue of *Fate* magazine contained an undated Bigfoot account that took place during the day on a desolate road near the town of Walhalla in Oconee County. The creature reported was a massive ten feet in height and the event was terrifying—in large part, because the witness was on foot. As the report states:

"I saw a gigantic, man-like creature. It was shaking the top of a small tree with one hand. It was 10 feet or more tall. He—it appeared to be male—had fur all over his body, and he had really big teeth. The creature's face was human, not ape-like.

I walked down the road toward the creature, not believing what I was seeing. I got within 45 feet of the thing. It looked at me and smiled the most terrifying smile I have ever seen. I stepped from the road and walked through the woods, afraid to look back."

Researcher Mary Green interviewed a woman who had a roadside sighting on Hwy 24 between the towns of Walhalla and Westminster in Oconee County. The incident occurred in late 1994 or early 1995 between one and three a.m.

It was a clear night, and the woman and her best friend

were driving back home after a visit to Cherokee, North Carolina.

As the woman was driving, she spotted something ahead in her headlights. It was clearly a living thing crossing the road, though she states that something about it didn't look normal. She slowed down, thinking perhaps it was a wounded animal. When the woman hit the brakes to slow down, the passenger also sat up at attention and looked ahead at the creature.

When they reached the thing, it had already crossed the highway and stopped on the passenger side of the road. As the witness drove past the creature, it stood looking at the vehicle.

The stunned women looked at each other, both asking what the thing was. The passenger was eager to turn around for a better look at the beast, but the driver refused.

The witness told Green that the creature's eyes reflected red and that its hair was bushy around the head. The thing also had hair all over its body. The hair on the creature's body, she notes, was short like a dog's fur.

The woman was especially disturbed by the creature's facial expression, as she recounted to Green:

"I saw a face...I saw a face, and I guess to the day I die, I will always see the face. And I don't believe those details will ever leave my mind, but that was...it just seemed to me, that there was so much hatred in the face...so much meanness in the eyes of whatever that was. That's what really sticks in my mind, is just the menacing look that was in that face."

The woman further clarified that the creature was definitely not a bear, had arms longer than a man's, and that its face had human-like features. She said the thing moved on all fours when it crossed the road and was somewhat gorilla-like. In hindsight, she still believes the creature was injured due to its odd movements.

The area of the sighting was heavily wooded and there were large apple orchards in the vicinity. There were few houses, and even those were spaced out sporadically in the area.

Many people have spotted Bigfoot along South Carolina highways.

On July 15, 1997, fourteen-year-old Jackie Hutto, saw a Sasquatch outside of his home in the small town of Neeses. It was around midday when the barking of the family dogs caught Jackie's attention. The dogs were inside a pen in the back yard, and when the boy went out to quiet them, he saw a creature pulling at the wire walls of the pen. Presumably, the thing was after the dogs.

What followed was like a scene from a movie. The creature looked at Jackie, at which point the boy screamed and made a run for the house. He glanced behind him only to see that the Bigfoot had turned and fled for the woods.

Jackie's sixteen-year-old brother, David, heard the commotion and rushed outside in time to catch a glimpse of the Bigfoot before it disappeared into the trees.

Jackie said the creature was 8 to 8 ½ feet tall and covered in black fur, except for its face, chest, and knees where brown skin could be seen. He also reported that the creature had teeth that were large, discolored and looked like "baby blocks."

Hutto also stated that the thing was a male, made clear by prominent genitalia, and that the creature was "really fat."

The brothers decided that the sighting should be reported,

so David made a call to the local newspaper, *The Times and Democrat* out of Orangeburg, South Carolina.

This, however, is where the account gets a bit questionable—in large part due to the choice David made when he spoke to a reporter. Instead of letting anyone know that the incident involved a young boy, David Hutto said that the witness, Jackie, was a twenty-three-year-old woman.

The following day, *The Times and Democrat*, reported the incident. Although no reporters had spoken with the imaginary woman, the news article included quotes from "Ms. Hutto."

"'I'm pretty sure he wanted to eat (the dogs) or something. I keep looking out the windows to make sure he's not out there. I'm a disbeliever—in a sense I still am. But I'm kinda having a change of heart,' Ms. Hutto said."

In short order, the story garnered a lot of attention and Bigfoot hunters were soon scouring the area looking for evidence of the creature. One woman voiced concern over "trigger happy Bigfoot hunters" roaming through the neighborhood.

It wasn't long before the Hutto brothers revealed that there was no "Ms. Hutto" who had spotted that beast and that the actual witness was a young boy. Reportedly, the boys lied in an attempt to remain anonymous. Of course, the attempt only hurt the credibility of the report and many people in the area thought the whole tale was a fabrication. The result was a lot of anger, much of it directed at the newspaper for running the story to begin with before checking their sources.

Other people took it all in stride, and some even tried to capitalize on the possibility of Bigfoot being in the area. Art Dent, owner of the Dog City Paint and Body Shop, put up an airbrushed sign that read "Big Foot Welcome Center."

Dent told reporters, "We don't want to hurt him. We want to feed him. He had to try to eat those dogs, because if he went in a restaurant he would get thrown out."

While Dent was clearly taking the matter tongue in cheek, others took a more serious approach. Concord, North Carolina, resident Brenda Polk was excited about the Hutto report because, for her, it was further evidence of what she already believed—that Bigfoot did indeed prowl the Carolinas.

Polk had her own sighting of the creature in 1991 near the South Carolina border. She told the *Times and Democrat*: "I'm trying to get a support group started for people in the Carolinas that have spotted Bigfoot and have a place for them to report without people telling them they've lost their mind."

Polk isn't afraid of the creatures, and when asked about the Hutto encounter, she responded:

"They won't attack anyone unless they are attacked. I don't think it's going to hurt anybody down there. They don't like dogs, and dogs don't like them. I've been studying it now for the past year. It has attacked dogs, but I haven't seen anywhere where it actually attacked humans other than when they harassed it."

Myrtle Beach's *Sun News* ran a story on the state's Bigfoot craze in its July 27, 1997, edition under the headline "Bitten by Bigfoot Bug." Following up on the Hutto story, reporter Pat Butler noted that strange things had been happening in Neeses for years. The small town, near the North Fork of the Edisto River, is believed by some to be a hotspot for Bigfoot.

Nineteen-year-old Cray Chavis, a Neeses resident, said that he hadn't seen a Bigfoot, but had seen other strange things in the town. He told Butler: "[There's] weird things around here. Like, it'd be light at night, and you see something run across the road in front of your car."

Other area residents say they know people who have spotted Bigfoot in the area but don't want to come forward with their sightings, some due to fear of ridicule, others just not wanting attention.

Butler noted that while some people believed the Hutto sighting was either a case of mistaken identity, or an outright fraud, others were sure the boys were being honest and that they really had seen a Bigfoot. Art Dent pointed out the rural nature of the area and the fact that kids were accustomed to the area's wildlife from an early age:

"When little boys grow up around here, when they get 4 or 5 years old, they don't get a bicycle or skateboard, they get a .22. They spend their whole lives hunting. If those boys said they saw something and it wasn't a deer, they probably saw something."

The *News* also spoke with Mary Harsey, a woman who lived near the Hutto home. Harsey said she was a believer in the hairy beast. "I wouldn't let the young'uns out for a couple of days. But if it's that big, it's gonna get us if it wants to get us," she said.

The paper also spoke with town secretary and treasurer Sonja Gleaton who said she wasn't sure what to think about a potential creature in the area. "I'm not saying I believe in Bigfoot, but I've got film in my camera, and I'm ready," she stated.

Pat Butler followed up with another Bigfoot article the following month. In the August 13 edition of *The State Newspaper*, Butler wrote about Tennessee Bigfoot researcher Rob McNabb and his efforts to track the creature in South Carolina.

McNabb noted that he had spoken with the Hutto brothers and found them to be credible witnesses. McNabb voiced his opinion that the Palmetto State was "unexplored territory, Bigfoot-wise."

McNabb himself had a Bigfoot sighting in the state. Although the paper doesn't list the date of the encounter or many details, it reports that the sighting occurred in Sumter County along US 378 while McNabb was on his honeymoon. No doubt it made for quite a wedding memory.

A report on the Jeff Rense Sightings Website details a roadside encounter that occurred in the spring of 1998.

It was sometime in May that a driver traveling on Highway 521 in Williamsburg County spotted a Bigfoot on the side of the road. The witness was between the towns of Andrews and Manning when the incident occurred.

The driver was headed home to Columbia at around 12

a.m. and saw something ahead of the vehicle standing on the right side of the road. As the witness observed, a small animal that looked like a fox ran across the highway. The animal was followed by something large, dark, and hairy that went leaping across the road behind the fox.

The witness was driving about 60 mph and swerved the car, worried about hitting the creature.

The beast had reddish-auburn hair that looked matted. The hair under the arms was a little lighter in color than the hair on the rest of the body. The creature was about six to seven feet tall. The witness further reports:

"Whatever it was, it was big and fast moving. I thought it might be a bear at first, but it seemed very man-like and kind of slender or lanky in a way, not round and thick like a bear. What really freaked me out was that its eyes caught and reflected the headlights so that they glowed as it went by. I'm just baffled by the whole event, and I was kind of spooked the rest of the way home."

The bipedal creature vanished into the trees and bushes on the left side of the road as the driver passed by.

The witness added a few other details about the incident:

"I had the vent on in the car and radio playing when I smelled something like a dead animal a little before I saw anything. The smell was almost like that of gangrene. It looked like it turned its head toward the car as it jumped. I saw two amber colored eyes, reflecting the headlights."

Sherman Carmichael chronicled a September 1998 Bigfoot sighting in his book *Mysterious South Carolina*. The creature in this case was spotted by an officer from Shaw Air Force Base in Sumter. The man was on his way home to North Myrtle Beach at the time and his two young sons were asleep in the back seat of the vehicle.

The sighting occurred around one a.m. The witness was near the town of Mullins in Marion County, just past the Little Pee Dee River on Highway 917.

As the driver passed the river, he noticed some kind of

animal in the ditch. Thinking at first it was a dog, the man slowed down to get a better look. He quickly realized that it wasn't a known animal. As Carmichael recounts:

"The animal stood up and looked in the direction of the oncoming car. When the lights hit it, it looked like it had an orangutan's face. There was no hair on the top of its head, and the body was covered in orange-brown hair. It did not appear to have a neck; it looked like the head just joined the shoulders. The witness could only see from about the waist up because it was standing in the roadside ditch. The chest area seemed much larger than its midsection."

The witness said that the ditch itself was three to four feet deep and that the creature was four to five feet above the top of the ditch. He thought the thing may have been eating a deer carcass or some other roadkill.

The creature's arms were very long, and the man saw what he took to be hands and fingers, leading him to believe that he was observing some kind of ape. He also noted that the creature's head was wider than normal and had "scraggly fur on top."

Bigfoot investigator Don Tart followed up on the man's sighting and examined the area of the encounter. Tart reports that there is sparse human population along the route and that it cuts through a vast section of swamp that is rich in resources. All in all, an excellent location for a large creature to hide out undetected.

The *Bigfoot Encounters* website has an account from a witness who reported two separate Bigfoot sightings. The man asked to remain anonymous and said that the encounters were in York County near Fort Mill.

The first sighting was in an open area with hardwood trees and cornfields on one side, and pines on the other side. One day in October 1999, the man spent a long day in a deer stand, arriving in the early morning hours and staying late. He hadn't seen anything all day and had decided to head home. As he was about to climb down from the stand, he heard a loud sound that he thought was possibly an owl. It sounded

close to his position, so he sat back down to try to determine what it was. He soon heard the sound again. He began trying to think of potential explanations—a large owl, or possibly even a panther were possibilities that ran through his head.

When he tried to shine a light in the direction of the sound, it stopped, and everything went silent. The witness related the incident to his brother, a wildlife biology student, who suggested the sound was some kind of big cat.

Whatever the case, the man hunted the spot four more times without incident. Then, the following season, he was back in the same tree stand and had a more dramatic experience. As he relates:

"I stayed in the stand late because I hadn't seen any deer and I wanted to see if possibly they had gone nocturnal on me, still nothing. So, I started down, untied my rifle, slung it across my shoulder, got my flashlight out of my pouch, turned around and poof, out of nowhere! I had not heard a thing. He, she, it was standing not 6 feet from me. My light hit it about halfway between its privates and its chest."

The witness was frozen in place. He wanted to look up but reports that he was afraid to make any movement, noting that he was too close to unshoulder his rifle for defense.

The creature made a movement as if crossing its arms and the hunter started running backwards as fast as possible. The Bigfoot made a deep sound and was gone as suddenly as it had appeared.

The witness says the creature was "large, human shaped, covered with black hair. Extremely large chest and forearm areas. I didn't see a face, only a large head outline."

The witness is a lifelong hunter and has spent a large amount of time in the woods. He has not returned to the area since his encounter.

2000s

Another report on the *Bigfoot Encounters* website concerns the observation of a seven-foot-tall creature in Union County in January 2001.

It was five a.m., and a small group of people were walking in the woods when they saw movement in a thicket. They stopped and stood still, waiting to see what was disturbing the brush. After about fifteen minutes, a bipedal creature emerged.

"It was much like a very large man but bigger. It didn't seem threatening, but it didn't know we were there. It was mostly black or very dark. It could have been brown, but it was very dark so hard to make out the color. It moved very slowly and did not make any sounds."

The reporting witness was sure the creature was not a bear and stated that the beast sat down for a portion of the time that the group watched it.

A hiker in the southeastern portion of the Francis Marion National Forest had seen a Bigfoot in the spring of 2002. The Berkeley County report was filed with the BFRO.

The incident took place somewhere between May 5-10. It was between 8-11 a.m., and the day was sunny and warm. The witness was looking down at the trail, watching for snakes, when something leapt across the path about 50 yards ahead. "It was on two legs, about the size of a person or bigger, and was uniform brown in color," the hiker reported.

The witness stopped and tried to process the sighting, thinking of all the potential explanations. Standing still and listening quietly revealed that there were no sounds from the woods and no indication of anyone or anything moving through the trees.

"I ruled out it was a person because it was all brown in color and had to be fur and not clothing. I knew it wasn't a deer because it was on two legs when it leaped across the trail. It was definitely a human shape though. After some thought, I decided to proceed forward up the trail where I saw this thing cross."

Nothing further was discovered and the witness notes that the narrow trail had thick trees on both sides.

A family observed a Bigfoot near the Catawba River in the summer of 2002. The BFRO report says the incident occurred on August 22 on Bethel Road near Highway 200 in Lancaster County.

The reporting witness was driving at around nine o'clock in the evening with her daughter, son, and grandson also in the vehicle. As the car rounded a curve, the driver spotted something ahead on the left side of the road. She moved to the opposite lane in order to avoid the figure. Once she passed it, her daughter commented that the thing looked like a gorilla. The driver also thought the creature looked like a gorilla.

"It stood upright without a slump like a gorilla. It ran in the same manner. It was maybe 5 ½ feet tall with a small head and broad shoulders. The color was solid black."

A woman driving in southern Cherokee County in April 2003 saw a massive creature cross the road ahead of her vehicle and she then observed it on a nearby hillside.

The woman was on her way to work and was traveling on Highway 105 near the town of Gaffney. It was around seven a.m. when she spotted movement on the road ahead. As she passed the spot, she looked up a small hill and saw a large, bipedal creature.

She reports that the creature was massive and had coarse hair that was 3 to 4 inches long. The witness says the beast had coloring similar to a gray fox or coyote.

The sighting occurred a few miles from the confluence of two waterways—the Broad River and the Pacolet River.

Bigfoot researcher Matt Pruitt spoke with the woman about the encounter. He writes:

"It was clearly upright and covered in coarse, charcoal gray hair. Interestingly, she stated that it had a section of hair on its chest that was nearly snow white. She likened the texture of the creature's hair to that of a yak. She kept emphasizing how massive the creature was, its chest being roughly three feet in breadth.

"She told me that she had no doubt that the creature she saw that morning was a Sasquatch."

Later the same day, on her way home from work, the woman stopped at the location where she had seen the creature. She notes:

"I went back after work but did not find tracks or disturbance of any kind. There was an overpowering smell. It smelled like fresh meat, like a meat locker."

In the fall of 2003, a pair of turkey farmers had a nighttime sighting in Chesterfield County, near the town of Jefferson. The reporting witness told the BFRO:

"My co-worker and I were on a turkey farm at about 12:30 a.m. one night in October 2003. I began smelling a strange smell that I had never smelled before on a bird farm. I began shining my Q-beam spotlight around in the darkness. I noticed something standing behind the barn across from me. I could see the animal picking up acorns or something off the ground. The animal didn't like my spotlight because it would block the light with its hand. I couldn't believe what I was seeing."

The man rushed to his co-worker and told him what he had seen, but the other man laughed it off, thinking that the witness was just trying to scare him. However, he soon learned differently. When he reached the spot himself, he shined his spotlight on the area and saw the same creature.

As the reporting witness states: "He claimed that this creature started walking toward him and it really shook him up because he ran to the front of his truck and sped to the front of the farm where I waited on him. He was white as a ghost. He claimed that the creature was between 8 to 10 ft. in height and as broad as two linebackers. I told him that's exactly what I had seen."

The Bigfoot had light brown shaggy hair and was estimated to be between 600 and 800 pounds.

According to the reporting witness, a similar creature

had been spotted three months prior on another turkey farm, three to four miles from his own sighting. He soon quit the job, being concerned about working at night with such a massive creature in the area.

A fall 2004 roadside sighting took place in the Francis Marion National Forest. The encounter took place on October 20 in Berkeley County near the town of Cordesville. The witness told the BFRO:

"It was just before dark, and I saw something ahead on all fours crossing the road. At first, I thought it was a horse, then a bear. It did not have a natural gait and the body was too thin to be a horse and it was too tall to be a bear. As I closed up on it, I saw that it had dark brown hair that was several inches long. The head was smaller than a horse or a bear. I believe it to be a Bigfoot on all fours."

The sighting took place around dusk. Conditions were clear and it was still fairly light. The driver was traveling on Highway 402 and stopped at the spot where the creature entered the woods, but nothing else was observed. The report states that the trees were very thick at the spot where the creature entered the woods. The witness estimates the Bigfoot was about nine feet in height.

BFRO investigator Leevon Patrick followed up with the witness and clarified that the creature had no visible tail, a flat back, and was all brown in color. The hair was long and hung six to eight inches off the body. Patrick further notes that after the man stopped to look around, he felt very uneasy and soon resumed his journey.

An anonymous report on the *Bigfoot Encounters* website tells of a sighting from Sumter County in early 2005. The report, posted on April 4, comes from a man who was hunting with two friends in a designated hunting area. The trio were each in separate tree stands but were in communication via 3-way radios. It was around 10:30 in the morning when all three heard an unusual grunting sound. Scanning the area, they spotted a large, dark creature standing out in the open.

"It was directly in the middle of the field. His arms were

bent back like the Bigfoot creature in the Patterson film, and it stood to about 8½ feet tall," the writer reported.

One of the hunters fired his rifle to frighten the creature and the men watched as it rushed away into the trees.

The reporting witness returned to the area the next day and photographed a large footprint in the area where the creature was seen.

A woman traveling on Highway 15 near Hartsville in Darlington County had a nighttime sighting in 2006 that gave her a fright.

The sighting was at 2:10 a.m. on March 13. The witness, a restaurant manager, told the BFRO that she was on her way home from work and almost hit a deer which shook her up and no doubt got her adrenaline flowing. As a result of the close call, she was extra alert as she continued her journey from Bishopville. When she saw another figure about 100 yards ahead in the road, she assumed it was another deer and slowed down. She soon discovered that it wasn't a deer, however. As she reports:

"I slowed my car down to about 30 to 40 mph to allow time for the animal to cross over. As I approached nearer to this shape, I noticed that it was human-like because it was standing erect on 2 legs and it had arms like a man; however, when I got within 40 ft. of this creature, I realized that it wasn't a bear or a deer and that it appeared to be very tall. I floored it...I was very afraid."

The witness reports that the creature's shoulders were above the top of her van, leading her to estimate that it was around eight feet tall. As she passed it, the thing seemed to lunge toward the vehicle, and it almost took off the side mirror.

The beast had a conical shaped head and no visible neck. The arms were long and massive and the legs muscular. The creature was covered in light colored hair that was four to five inches in length. The entire incident left the woman very shaken.

Interestingly, she notes that growing up in Hartsville,

she'd heard stories of people seeing Bigfoot in the area for a long time. Her grandmother told her that a family member had seen one of the creatures in the 1920s.

Hartwell Dam, location of a 2007 encounter.

A man fishing in Anderson County in late spring 2007 had a strange experience near Lake Hartwell Dam.

It was Friday, June 1, and the witness was on the Savannah River between Lake Hartwell and Lake Russel on the South Carolina/Georgia border. He had started fishing around eight in the evening hoping to catch some trout or walleye. He was ready to call it quits just after nine when he heard the sound of footsteps approaching him. He first thought it was another fisherman coming down the same trail he had used, but he quickly realized the sounds were coming from up the side of a hill.

As the figure got closer, the man became concerned and opened the thumb snap on his sidearm. He shined his LED headlamp in the direction of the steps, and when he did so, the sound stopped. There was nothing to be seen, no eyeshine nor sign of any animal.

The witness was very concerned at this point and headed

back to the safety of his truck. Whatever it was in the trees walked parallel to him all the way to the parking area.

Once in his vehicle, he turned on a larger light and shined it into the woods hoping to see what was there, but he still couldn't find the source of the footsteps.

The witness reports that he had spent his life in the woods and was confident that it wasn't a deer.

"I don't know if it could have been a Bigfoot...all I know is the whole thing was very strange because usually a deer or other animals will spook when you put a light on them."

BFRO investigator Don Tart followed up on the incident and made several trips to the area himself. On one of his treks, Tart also heard something unidentified walking parallel to him along the trail.

"The area is ripe for activity," Tart states. "The woods are deep, and ridges with rocky crags run right down to the river. This area of the state is sparsely inhabited and there is a good mix of hardwoods and pine forests with rolling hills. The climate is mild. Fish and game are plentiful."

Tart also reports that other people fishing in the area have had experiences similar to the reporting witness. Hunters who have spent time in the region have reported hearing wood knocks and unexplained howls in the night.

A newspaper carrier had an early morning sighting in Dorchester County in the winter of 2007. The sighting occurred on a Sunday morning in January at 6:45 near the town of Ridgeville.

The man was near the end of his route. He had just put a paper in a box and pulled forward to deliver the next one when his headlight caught something off to his far left. He watched closely and saw a tall figure walking along the tree line at the edge of a cornfield. At first, he thought the figure was a man, but he quickly realized that it was all black, and, as he watched, the figure looked in his direction. At that point, the witness observed red eyes staring at him. The thing then continued to walk away, and the man turned his vehicle to try to get a better look at the figure. The action caught the creature's attention and it stopped to look back at the witness before turning and continuing to walk away.

The man estimated the creature was between six and seven feet tall. Due to lighting and environmental conditions, he could not see the face well enough to get a description, though he stated that the head appeared pointed.

The BFRO report on the matter notes that the area is very rural, has a lot of farmlands, and is surrounded by dense woodlands.

The witness reports that he is familiar with bear and other wildlife from the region, and he is adamant that what he observed was not a bear. He felt as if he had disturbed the creature and when it stopped and stared at him, the man felt intimidated. He reports feeling "spooked" and drove away from the area quickly after the sighting.

The *Charleston City Paper* reported on Bigfoot in its February 15, 2012, edition, under the headline "Sasquatch Investigators Keep the Faith Alive."

The article, by writer Paul Bowers, begins with a report from Mary Beth Pope who had a Bigfoot sighting in November 2007 while out in the Sumter National Forest. Pope was with four fellow members of the BFRO when she heard leaves and twigs crunching nearby. She looked to her left and saw an eight-foot-tall creature walking alongside her about thirty feet away. The creature had shaggy fur and long arms that swung down by its knees.

Pope resumed walking, not wanting the creature to run off. She said that when she started walking again, so did the Bigfoot. Pope focused on a meadow ahead and knew that the team was reaching the end of their hike. She wanted to get to the meadow and be close to the others. Before she reached the clearing, the creature took off in a different direction and vanished into the forest.

Pope runs a sustainable food wholesale and retail business on Pawleys Island, but on the side, she spends her time researching Bigfoot as an investigator with the BFRO. Pope doesn't worry about convincing people that the creatures are real. She states: "For me, I don't feel like I have to convince anyone, because I know what I saw."

A motorist traveling on Highway 61 in Colleton County spotted a Bigfoot in the spring of 2009.

On May 2, at 8:10 in the morning, the witness was about halfway between the towns of Canady and Givhans, near the Edisto River, when he spotted what he took to be a man walking on the side of the road ahead of him.

Although he could see only a silhouette, he assumed it was a man going to check a mailbox across the road. He began to slow down, concerned that the man might step back into the road without looking for traffic. His shock came when he reached the spot and realized there was no man visible, no mailbox, and not even a house in sight! There were thick woods on both sides of the road and nowhere for anyone to hide.

"I began thinking about what I had really seen. He had walked up to the road from the right in a leisurely manner, what I call a mosey. When he stepped into the road his first stride put him in the center of my lane His second step put him at the center line. He crossed the road in four steps and at no time during this did the sun show between his legs above the knee.

"This was a big man. His hands swung in front and behind his body as he walked. There was nothing in his hands. A hunter would have had a gun or a bow with him. I could see no color distinction between any parts of his body."

The witness returned to the spot the following day and walked up and down the area, trying to understand what he had seen, but he could find no explanation for his sighting.

A witness told the GCBRO (Gulf Coast Bigfoot Research Organization) about a January 14, 2012, incident in Allendale County. The reporting witness was driving through a swampy area around 11:30 at night and spotted what looked like "a pair of apes standing by the side of the road."

The witness said the creatures looked like apes down on their front knuckles. They reportedly had very dark, short hair with massive upper bodies and long arms. The driver estimated the creatures in the 600-to-700-pound range.

My files contain a similar report from a woman who said she'd seen a large gorilla while driving through a swampy area of Allendale County in March 2013. The woman, who preferred to remain anonymous, said she was driving home from a trip. Around midnight, she spotted something ahead on the side of the road. Thinking it was an animal and wanting to be cautious in case it ran in front of her car, she proceeded carefully. As she slowly passed the creature, she got a good look at it:

"It looked a lot like a big gorilla to me. Pointed head, large chest and big arms. And it looked pissed off. It was glaring at me and all I could think was, 'I'm in its territory.' I hit the gas and got out of there."

L to R—South Carolina researcher Mike Richburg, Cryptozoologist Lyle Blackburn, Author, Jeff Byers.

Mike Richburg, whose early Bigfoot encounter is covered under the 1970s section of this book, has collected many reports from South Carolina over the years. Mike's own sighting when he was a teenager had a long-lasting effect on him, causing him to stay out of the woods for years because of the intense encounter. He eventually overcame his fear and has since had other experiences during his own investigations.

In 2012, Richburg had another encounter, only thirty miles from the first incident. It was late spring, and Mike was on a daytime hike through the woods of Sparkleberry Swamp. Located on upper Lake Marion, Sparkleberry is part of the Upper Santee Swamp system, a 1,600-acre area teeming with wildlife. The resource rich region is near the confluence of the Congaree and Wateree Rivers and Mike planned to set out a game camera in hopes of catching an image of Bigfoot.

While Mike had seen some unusual things in his years of research, nothing had come close to his initial sighting of a Bigfoot in 1978. Still, like many researchers, he hoped to one day catch a clear image of one of the creatures on film.

Moving through the Sparkleberry Swamp that day, Richburg had to cross a creek with a high bank. He moved carefully down the bank and started wading through the water toward the opposite side. He heard what he assumed were two animals moving around above him up the embankment. The vegetation was thick and as Richburg focused on the area of the sounds, he saw an animal suddenly dart out from cover and move away at great speed. Mike couldn't believe his eyes. It was a massive, ape-like creature completely covered in dark hair, just like the thing he had seen in 1978. As he watched, the creature ran about eighty yards from the creek.

"It was running on all fours in a real funny manner because its arms were so big. Its chest sort of bobbed up a couple of times, then on the third bob, it went bipedal."

Richburg watched in shock as the creature ran and switched from a four-legged run to two legs in one fluid movement. It was mindboggling that such a large creature could move so quickly. Richburg noted that the thing was fast enough to "easily run down a deer."

In seconds, the creature had vanished into the trees. Mike

was stunned and a bit disappointed. He had not mounted his game camera when the thing appeared, and tucked in his pack was an 8mm camera, one that he'd had no chance to take out since the sighting had happened so suddenly.

A 2014 article in Columbia's *Free-Times* newspaper on February 9, 2014, detailed the search for Bigfoot in the upstate portion of South Carolina. Writer Eva Moore spent time with Cari and Chris George during their search for the creature in a wooded area in Oconee County. Moore writes:

"We're in Upstate South Carolina. But I can't tell you exactly where we are today because photographer Sean Rayford and I agreed to sign a nondisclosure agreement. The Georges want to protect Bigfoot."

The Georges told Moore that they were concerned about people hunting Bigfoot with a goal of shooting one of the creatures. The concern was due in large part to Spike television's "10-million-dollar bounty" on the creature. It was all part of a reality TV show revolving around the hunt for conclusive proof of the existence of Bigfoot. While some thought the program was "good television," others found it a complete farce in poor taste. Either way, the series only lasted for a single season.

The Georges, along with Chris' parents, Marty and Lisa George, are some of the founding members of a group known as the Carolina Cryptid Crew, a team dedicated to the search for unknown animals in the Carolinas.

Moore is clear that she's not a believer, noting that she thinks an animal as large as Bigfoot in North America would have been found already. Still, she does give the Georges time to report some of their findings.

The team has discovered footprints, heard wood knocks and howls, and found "tree structures" that they believe were created by Bigfoot.

Cari also shared a personal experience with the reporter. As the article states:

"It was during the summer. Chris was laid up on the

couch, and Cari and her in-laws were out looking for evidence.

"'We were walking,' she says. 'My mother-in-law stops: she says, 'There's a tree moving' Then her mother-in-law saw a flash of red, she says.

"Was she scared?

"'My adrenaline was going because I've been interested in Bigfoot since I was a little girl, Cari says. 'I thought they were all in Washington. I didn't think I'd ever see one.'"

Cari told the reporter that she and her mother-in-law went in one direction and her father-in-law went in another. In moments, she saw the creature. As she relates:

"I just stop—because this creature steps out of the trees, looks at me, turns around, walks a bit, turns around again, looks at me, and it's like it was saying 'Don't follow me.' And I was just kind of frozen. Then it just walked on and disappeared in the trees."

Cari says the creature was about seven foot tall and completely covered in hair. She wasn't frightened and she's unsure why she didn't think to take a photo—she had a camera in her hand, but she never snapped the shutter. She told the paper:

"I just couldn't do it. It's just mystical and you never think you're going to see one. When that happens, you're not prepared.

"You think if you see one it's going to look like Harry and the Hendersons. It wasn't like that. It was like a teddy bear. Very friendly looking. It had some white on its face, but it was nothing like what I expected. It looked more like an Ewok."

On May 5, 2015, CBS news mentioned a bizarre incident from Wadmalaw Island. A dog was found impaled alive on a tree limb fifteen feet in the air! Officials suggested the animal "ran up a tree while chasing an animal."

The absurd explanation didn't sit well with many people who suspected that some unusual creature such as a Bigfoot was responsible for the terrible state of the dog.

A man in McClellanville said he encountered an aggressive Bigfoot in 2016 and the creature wasn't by itself—a smaller one was with it at the time.

The witness sent in a report to the *Phantoms and Monsters* website about the incident. He said that he and his wife were moving a table and lawn chairs into their garage when he saw a pair of hairy figures walking through the trees about a hundred feet from his position.

The larger creature must have sensed that the man was watching because it stopped walking and turned to look at the witness.

The man had a clear view and realized he was looking at a Bigfoot. After a few seconds, the creature shook its head, let out a grunt, and started walking towards the witness.

The man quickly slammed the door shut and locked it behind him. His wife had not observed the creatures and was puzzled by her husband's behavior. The man reported:

"The big one was very tall, I'd say over 8 foot and huge. It was covered in ruddy brown hair and had a dark colored face. The other one was a few feet shorter. I don't think I've ever been so scared. I've never seen anything like that in these woods or anywhere in this area. We've lived here for 27 years, and I know the outdoors well."

The witness investigated the area the following morning, but no tracks or other evidence was visible. He speculated that the rain had obscured any tracks left by the creatures.

As more people become involved in the search for Bigfoot, there's no doubt that more and more accounts will surface from the Palmetto State. In the long run, it may be one of the quiet, unexpected places that yields some significant proof of the creature's existence.

A long-haul trucker spotted a Sasquatch in Berkeley County in the spring of 2021.

The trucker filed a report with the BFRO and noted that the sighting occurred in March while he was driving a load of steel coils from Canada to the Nucor Steel plant.

The man was driving southwest on Cainhoy Road when he spotted a creature standing in the woods on the right side of the road. Since it was early spring, there were few leaves on the trees and the man had a good view of the creature. He reported that it was massive with broad shoulders and a powerful build. The man reports:

"I witnessed a 8-9 ft tall upright hominoid creature with black hair and brownish grey skin apparent on its face and chest and abdomen. There was also noticeable scraggly matted hair hanging from its arms. It had wide bold shoulders and hair partly covering its forehead. The eyes were wide set and large."

The man did not stop his truck due to high standing water on the sides of the road.

PALMETTO STATE MONSTERS by David Weatherly

PART FOUR
Strange South Carolina Legends

Strange South Carolina

Strange things seem to abound in South Carolina. From weird legends of the Lowcountry, to out of place or unusually large-sized animals. Curiously, several Palmetto State natives have mentioned the 2.5 size phenomenon. In short, this is the idea or belief that some things in South Carolina often grow two and a half times beyond their normal size.

Mike Richburg mentions incredibly large tomatoes, for instance. Another gentleman told me that vegetables from his garden frequently grew well beyond their normal range.

The concept extends to animals too. People have reported unusually sized domestic animals as well as wild specimens, including birds and snakes.

While the phenomenon doesn't appear to be consistent, there are enough cases to make it, at the least, a curiosity. No one seems to have an explanation as to why this is the case, and, of course, no official studies have been conducted to determine if there is some environmental condition that creates the effect.

But beyond this, the Palmetto State offers plenty of other odd legends from its early days to present times, as we shall see here.

Flying Serpents & Giant Birds

If we are to believe reports out of South Carolina from the late 1800s, a flying serpent or two zipped through the skies over the state. From the May 31, 1888, edition of the *Dunkirk Observer Journal* comes this account:

"Columbia, May 31—There comes a story from Darlington County, this State, of a flying serpent.

"Monday evening just before sunset Miss Ida Davis and her two younger sisters were strolling through the woods when they were suddenly startled by the appearance of a huge serpent moving through the air above them. The uncanny creature was distant only two or three rods when they first beheld, and was sailing through the air with a speed equal to that of a hawk or buzzard, but without any visible means of propulsion. Its movements and its flight resembled those of the snake and looked a formidable object as it wound its way along, being apparently about 15 feet in length and as large around as a good-sized human thigh.

"The girls stood amazed and followed it with their eyes until it was lost to view in the distance. The flying serpent was also seen by a number of people in another part of the country early in the afternoon of the same day, and by these it is represented as admitting a hissing noise, which could distinctly be heard. The [African American] population in that section are greatly excited over the matter. Religious revival meetings have been inaugurated in their churches, and many of them declare that the day of judgment is near at hand."

The bizarre creature, or one like it, seems to have returned nine years later since we find another report of a flying snake from the state. This time, the *Branford Opinion* covered the story in its August 7, 1897, edition. Under the headline "A Flying

Snake is Reported from South Carolina," the paper reports:

"The Hartsville correspondent of *The News and Courier* describes it in detail as follows:

"The flying snake was seen near Newman swamp by a Mr. Odom on Sunday afternoon, at 6 o'clock. This is about ten miles south of this place. Later, say 7 o'clock on the same day, it was seen by Mr. Henry Polson, in Chesterfield County, twelve miles north of here. Mr. Polson says: 'The monster was low down, just above the treetops; had its head thrown back in position to strike and was just floating through the atmosphere lengthwise.' He says it seemed to be twenty-five to forty feet long and about eight to ten inches through at the largest part. In the language of Mr. Polson, 'He do not say it was a snake, but he do say it was the most like a snake of anything he ever saw, and he believes it was a snake.'

"There are all kinds of opinions as to what the monster could be. Everyone in lower Chesterfield almost is giving out an opinion, but the most original explanation is from my friend, William J. Johnson, a near neighbor of Mr. Polson. He says it was surely the devil going on to Washington to look after Ben Tilman and the Tariff Bill. Mr. Johnson says the snake was seen near Chesterfield courthouse and also in several towns in North Carolina."

Do giant birds soar over South Carolina?

A more modern account of a strange, winged creature comes from South Carolina cryptid researcher Mike Richburg who encountered a giant bird that sent a chill up his spine.

It was a warm September day in 1989 in South Carolina's Lowcountry. Richburg was driving a truck in the early morning hours when the incident occurred. Two other people were with him, his wife at the time, and his best friend. The trio was on their way for a camping trip, and both passengers were sleeping while Mike drove them all to their destination.

Mike thought it was going to be a pleasant country drive as he headed southbound on Highway 21. Little did he know what was in store for him on the road ahead.

The area at the time was very rural. Simple South Carolina country roads with lots of forests and wildlife. Most of the highway consisted of long, straight stretches with occasional curves. Mike told me how the incident unfolded:

"I'm running about 55-60 miles an hour at most. It's the early morning and I know there's going to be a lot of deer out, I'm not trying to hit one of those. I came to a kink in the road and then hit a long straightaway. There's nothing but big, thick trees on each side of the road, and I see, way up ahead, what looks like the white tails of some deer bouncing in the road."

As he continued moving toward the object ahead, Mike's eyes focused in, trying to determine exactly what was ahead. As the object began to take shape, his mind processed the possibilities. The object was too big to be a deer or a dog. "Strange as it sounds, I started thinking it looked like a horse with a tarp over it," he told me.

Richburg started to slow his truck down as he continued to focus in on what was ahead. The sudden realization of what he was looking at sent a chill through him.

"It was a bird. A huge bird. It was brown like the color of a golden eagle, but it was massive, and it was standing on a deer carcass. That thing looked at me straight in the eye and it was not a comfortable feeling. It hopped around, then showed its back to me, then it cocked its wings."

Mike quickly rolled the window up, not knowing what the giant raptor might do. Then he reached over and started furiously shaking his passengers, shouting at them to wake up and look out to the road ahead.

"I knew somebody else had to see that thing or they'd just think I was crazy. Then it opened its wings. One wingtip was over the center line of the highway, the other wingtip was over the grass on the side of the road. The wingspan was at least 16-18 feet."

Richburg's passengers were now awake, looking at the creature in shock. As the trio watched, the bird took flight, cycling its wings three times to clear the area. The giant bird carried the deer carcass off into the sky, flying away toward the still rising sun.

"I think that deer had some light fawn spots, but still, it was a good 40–50-pound animal that bird carried off, that ain't no easy thing to do."

The witnesses watched in awe as the bird flew away into the distance. Mike's friend said it looked like a hang glider with a full-grown man on it. None of them had ever seen such a sight.

Mike told me that he'd seen patches of white on the inside of the bird's wings when they opened. With the Combahee River running parallel to the highway, and an abundance of wildlife in the region, a large predator could certainly thrive in the area. Mike also noted the size and appearance of the bird's legs:

"The legs looked really weird to me, they were big as tree trunks and rough looking. I realized later what it probably was—in that region, that bird would be standing in black mud when it got water. I bet its legs were covered with dried mud that had cracked, giving it that appearance."

In *Mysterious South Carolina*, Sherman Carmichael reports a spring 2009 incident involving a man driving on Highway 601 headed toward Bamberg. The driver purportedly saw a massive bird. According to the account:

"The bird had very long tail feathers, a wingspan of about 15 feet, and a very large body. The bird had white and blue feathers, a short, pointed beak, and a plume on its head. The giant bird flew within three hundred yards of the driver and was about 30 to 40 ft above the ground."

It was around nine or ten in the morning and conditions were clear at the time of the sighting. The area was mostly open farmland along both sides of the highway, so the area was clear, and it was easy for the driver to observe the bird as it flew from one side of the road to the other.

Curiously, the same man claims to have seen a similar bird on another occasion while driving toward the town of Denmark. This time, the bird was smaller with an estimated wingspan of about eight feet. Like the first sighting, this bird was reportedly blue and white in color.

It's possible, of course, that the man spotted a known bird that he was simply unfamiliar with or that isn't native to the region. Estimating the size of airborne objects is not easy, especially for untrained observers.

A man in South Carolina's Lowcountry told me he'd seen a bird that looked like an eagle but twice the size of a normal eagle, flying over his father's property in 2017. The bird never landed so there was nothing to compare the creature's size to and he never spotted it again.

Numerous witnesses say panthers live in the Palmetto State.

Big Cats

Beyond stories of Bigfoot, one of the most persistent cryptozoological legends involves big cats. From mysterious, out of place lions and tigers, to the infamous black panthers, big cats are reported far and wide. The topic is one that irritates wildlife officials, but keeps locals talking, firm in their knowledge of what they know they saw.

Roger Pinckney, writing for *Sporting Classics Daily* on January 31, 2020, put it perfectly:

"Panther, painter, catamount, puma, wampus cat, mountain lion, *Puma concolor*—it's the most widely distributed land mammal in the New World, from Patagonia to the wilds of the Yukon. A foot longer than a man is tall, a big tom will tip 200 pounds. Paws as big as Waffle House waffles, fangs you don't want to fool with. Call it the Ghost Cat, too. What in the world did I just see? They appear and disappear like swamp-ground haints. They have been in South Carolina since the successful conclusion of the last Ice Age, but no longer. And why not? Because the US Fish and Wildlife Service says so."

Historical accounts mention big cats in the Palmetto State and reports go back to the early days of European exploration. Take the record of John Lawson, for instance.

Lawson was a wealthy young man who set out to explore the Carolinas in the early 1700s. Along his thousand-mile trek through both North and South Carolina, he collected notes and details of his experiences, which were published in 1709 as *A New Voyage to Carolina*. One account in the book records the sighting of a big cat. As Lawson recounts:

"As we were on our road this morning, our Indian shot at a Tyger [sic] that cross'd our way, he being a great distance from us. I believe he did him no harm because he sat on his Breech afterwards, and look'd upon us. I suppose he expected to have had a Spaniel Bitch, that I had with me, for his breakfast, who ran towards him, but Midway stopt her Career, and came sneaking back to us with her tail betixt her legs."

It's initially unclear exactly what kind of big cat Lawson spotted, though given the time period it would seem likely it was an eastern cougar. The curious point is that he refers to it as a tiger, implying that it had stripes or patterning on its coat. Michael Mayes clarifies an important point about the account in his own book *Shadow Cats: The Black Panthers of North America*. Mayes writes:

"Some scholars believe that Lawson misspoke when he called the cat in question a "tyger" and that he had really seen a mountain lion. Recall that the terms tyger, tiger, Mexican lion, and Mexican tiger, were often used to describe jaguars from the 1700s to the early 1900s."

Mayes points to another passage from Lawson as further proof that the explorer knew the difference between the two species. Lawson writes:

"Tygers are never met withal in the settlement; but are more to the Westward and are not numerous on this side of the Chain of Mountains. I once saw one that was larger than a Panther and seemed to be a very bold Creature. The Indians that hunt in those Quarters, say, they are seldom met withal. It seems to differe [sic] from Tyger of Asia and Africa."

The passage gives clear indication that Lawson was familiar with both types of big cat as well as where they were likely to be found.

In *Creatures on the Outer Edge*, Loren Coleman and Jerome Clark mention a sighting of what could have been a female lion.

The encounter occurred in 1948 in the White Oak Swamp. Sam Lee, manager of Rice Hope Plantation, and a companion, Troy T. Rogers, were out around 10:30 at night looking to catch poachers.

The pair had gotten out of their truck when they heard an

odd sound. Lee turned on his flashlight and illuminated a big cat that looked like a "mane less lion." The cat reared up slowly and stood on its hind legs, staring at the men at eye level.

Lee was armed with a small .22 caliber rifle which likely seemed puny in the face of the big cat. Rogers had already retreated to the safety of the truck and Lee quickly followed suit.

The town of Yemassee was disturbed by a "prowling terror" in 1957. The beast was spotted by hunters in late August and several other locals quickly followed up and reported their own sightings. The creature was described as about five feet long with a four-foot, bushy tail. Witnesses said the thing also emitted a high-pitched wail.

Police Chief Earl Youmans said that he and his officers were on the lookout for the creature, but he expressed the opinion that people were mistaken in their descriptions, claiming that the creature had "been built up into something that just doesn't exist."

Orangeburg, SC, paper *The Times and Democrat* reported on the beast in their September 5 edition under the banner "Yellow Monster May Be Panther."

"Yemassee's yellow monster with the scream of a woman probably is nothing more than a good size panther," the paper reported, based on comments from Chief Youmans.

The opinion gained more weight a few days later when Sgt. S. B. Hall of the state highway patrol was out hunting with a friend. The pair spotted the creature and reported that it was definitely a panther.

New York, NY's *Daily News* reported on the return of the "Dixie Demon" in its April 27, 1958, edition. The paper said the beast had been roaming through the South for five years and had ranged from Bladenboro, North Carolina, to Yemassee, South Carolina. The creature was described as a large, black panther that "cried like a baby."

A man named Tommy Baysden saw a pair of panthers in 1978, one adult and one cub. Two other witnesses were with him, and they watched the animals move over a rice field dike.

In 1980, a man named Lee Gray saw a black panther on Palmetto Bluff, just off the New River. Gray was fishing from a boat and watched the "big, black tom" crossing a deadfall pine across a rice canal.

One man told me he'd seen a "dark, tawny-colored panther" near the South Carolina/Georgia border in 1996. The witness was of the opinion that the cat was a Florida panther that had made its way up from the Sunshine State.

Another man told me he'd seen a big cat in the same region in 2004. This one, however, was of the black panther variety.

What's interesting about the accounts is that they both occurred around the Sumter National Forest in the Northwest portion of the state. The forest covers an area of 370,442 acres, is rich in natural resources, and could be prime territory for undiscovered or rare animals to hide out. The Sumter National Forest is also in the corner of the state close to the borders of both Georgia and North Carolina. If Florida panthers are indeed trekking up to the mountains, it would certainly seem a likely location for them.

The sightings are examples of what locals say are indicative of many more accounts, accounts that most outdoorsmen stay quiet about. After all, why bother to report the incidents when wildlife officials deny the existence of the cats?

Patty Kennedy, director of a conservancy in the state, reported that ten big cat sightings were logged in 2008 alone. Most were of the black panther variety. The conservancy group set out game cameras hoping to catch images of the cats but had no luck.

The state's wildlife agency conducted a five-year study that concluded in 2011. Based on their findings, they officially declared that the eastern cougar had been extinct since the 1930s. If officials hoped that the document would quell reports, they were likely disappointed because residents continue to log accounts of phantom cats.

The same year the study was completed, a man named Bill

Hameza spotted a pair of tawny colored panthers. The incident occurred in November while the man was out on a hunting trip in Colleton County. The hunter estimated the size of the cats to be about one hundred pounds each. Hameza believed they were both juveniles.

An even more unusual big cat sighting came from a man named Howard Hart. Hart was making a late-night run (date unknown) to pick up a load of crabs for Golden Harbor Seafood in Yemassee. He was shocked when a panther crossed the road in front of his truck. He said the animal was skinny and sickly looking and possibly had mange. Hart related the incident to his employer, Charlie Marshall, but Marshall brushed it off, thinking that Hart had been drinking. Marshall changed his tune the next night, however, when he made the run himself and had his own sighting. Marshall apparently saw the same panther, but this time, it had several spotted cubs walking behind it.

On February 12, 2019, a story broke about a man who was attacked by a black panther. It hit the news and spread quickly across social media and Internet sites.

The man, thirty-three-year-old Rickey Wesley Lynch of Hemingway, told officials the cat attacked and dragged him down by his pant leg, then drug him into a ditch.

Lynch also claimed to have seen a cub that crossed his path just before the larger cat attacked.

Apparently, the cat lost interest and trotted away before doing further damage to the man, though when Lynch called 911, he said the animal was sitting nearby making what he described as "crying sounds."

Lynch had superficial wounds that included a pair of scratch marks on his right leg and a single scratch mark on his right arm. An ambulance arrived at the scene and took him to the hospital for treatment. Meanwhile, Georgetown deputies spent what was described as an "hours-long search" for the mysterious black cat and the Department of Natural Resources was brought in to investigate.

In short order, the truth came out—Lynch had fabricated

the story. The man's motivations for doing so weren't clear, but officials were not amused and charged him with filing a false police report and breach of peace.

My files do contain a number of other big cat sightings in the state; unfortunately, most of them are very scant on details and often consist of someone saying that they spotted a massive wild cat.

As is the case in many other states, officials deny the possibility of large cats in the wild, and locals quietly talk to each other about the frequent reports. Whether the cats are surviving eastern cougars or something else unknown remains to be seen.

Some people thought that the beast that terrified a community in 1972 may have been a big cat, but the case had many puzzling aspects. Whatever it was, it left an impression on the people of Summerton.

Big Cats

The Thing of '72

The people of Summerton in Clarendon County experienced a series of unusual and disturbing events in early 1972. First, there was a series of earthquake tremors that rattled the area and put residents on edge. But the other incidents were something far stranger. A mysterious series of pet and livestock deaths took place in the community. Something, some "thing" was on the loose in the area and no one seemed to know exactly what it was.

One newspaper called it the Spook of Summerton, but many locals simply referred to it as The Thing.

The January 12 edition of the *Sumter Daily Item* called the creature The Thing and reported that it was a "beast without mercy ravaging the Summerton Area." Staff writer Van King wrote about the incidents in the *Item*:

"What will it kill next? Whatever it is, this throat-gouging, neck-breaking, fence jumping terror has got some Summerton folks a little worried. Murder, whether of a man or beast, is not a pleasant subject."

It was bad enough that a phantom predator was roaming the area, but it wasn't just the creature's elusive nature that had folks concerned. The animal seemed to possess abilities that bordered on the supernatural.

Bill DuBose, Summerton's superintendent of public utilities, lost a number of goats to the beast. DuBose had put the animals in an area that was surrounded by an eight-foot wire fence topped with three strands of barbed wire, yet somehow, The Thing got to the animals. DuBose went out one morning and was disturbed to find six of the seven animals had been killed. Each one had two deep fang marks in their throats.

DuBose reported that the seventh goat had completely vanished, presumably carried off by the creature. But what could get over an eight-foot-high fence and barbed wire? Especially while carrying one of its victims?

Clarendon County Sheriff T.J. Jackson was just as puzzled as everyone else. "I don't know what it is," he stated. "Some folks say it's a giant bobcat or lion, but I can't see how even a mighty big cat could get over a fence that high and carry off an entire goat. Everybody's kind of looking and listening now. This thing has kind of baffled me."

Large tracks were found at the site where the goats were attacked and killed. Bill DuBose thought the killer was a "South Carolina Panther." He found prints that measured at least five inches wide, though they were almost washed out by rain. As sure as he said he was of the creature's identity, even he couldn't explain some aspects of the attacks. As the *Daily Item* reported:

"The superintendent, along with a lot of other folks, is still trying to figure out how it jumped the imposing fence to get to the goats. There are several other unanswered questions that arouse the imagination. Where is the seventh goat? Did The Thing eat it, or did it somehow drag it from the enclosure? Why does The Thing kill, leaving only two deep fang marks without eating the victims?"

Two days after the death of the goats, Woody Corbett of Summerton, lost his favorite bird-dog to the beast. The animal was killed in the same manner with punctures to the throat. The dog may have put up a fight though. Corbett reported that the animal had deep gashes on its back and hips, and its neck had been broken.

A report of a strange sighting the previous year led many people to believe the beast had been spotted before by a pair of Manning residents. The men, Billy Hilton and Bill King, were driving in the Smythe Woods area one evening when they saw an unusual creature. Hilton reported:

"I saw what looked like a tremendous bobcat, bigger than a German shepherd and colored like a taffy cat. It was crossing I-95. It jumped the ditch and the fence, all in one leap, with grace gone to bed. It looked long and narrow, about five feet long, and it was higher in the back than it was in the front."

The men weren't sure how wide the area was that the beast leapt, but Hilton estimated the jump was between 30 and 40 feet.

There was plenty of speculation about The Thing's identity, but no logical possibilities matched the killer's profile. State wildlife officials and seasoned outdoorsmen didn't know what the creature was either. W.F. Robey Jr., writing for *South Carolina Wildlife magazine*, speculated that the almost extinct puma might be residing in South Carolina. The puma is certainly a strong contender for The Thing's identity, but the deaths didn't match a big cat's habits. Big cats kill for survival and eat their prey, but The Thing, whatever it was, almost seemed to kill for pleasure and left corpses strewn about uneaten.

Locals had been reporting strange cats in the area for some time prior to the attacks. The *Daily Item* noted:

"Over the year, hunters have talked about seeing giant bobcats, pumas, panthers, and other unexplained predators in the swamps of the Carolina Lowcountry."

Still, Summerton's Thing remained a mystery. The deaths trickled off and stopped, and people were left to wonder if the beast had completely departed the area, or if it was taking a break. Even today, when the occasional animal disappears, those who remember The Thing wonder if it has returned.

Historic Newberry, home of the Hound of Goshen.

The Hound of Goshen

The small town of Newberry, in Newberry County, is a scenic place rich in history. It was a thriving center for trade from the 1850s into the 1860s when the railroad and cotton were cornerstones of commerce.

Newberry still has southern charm with a current population of around ten thousand people. Like many towns, it has its own unique legend, one that involves a ghostly white hound.

The Hound of Goshen, also known as the Ghost Hound of Goshen, is a large white dog with glowing red eyes that lurks on a five mile stretch of road. The animal is aggressive and known to chase travelers who tread into its territory.

The legend of the ghost hound begins in the 1850s when a peddler arrived in town to sell his wares. The traveling salesman was accompanied by a large white dog that constantly stayed by his side.

Soon after the peddler was in town, there was a murder. Being the only stranger around, suspicions fell on the man. He was, very much, in the wrong place at the wrong time.

An angry mob, positive that the salesman was guilty of the crime, took matters into their own hands and lynched the man. His loyal dog tried to protect him and as the man was being strung up, the dog started biting members of the mob. One man turned a rifle on the dog and took a shot. He either missed, or only grazed the dog, because it ran from the scene and escaped, disappearing into the woods.

The peddler fell victim to the mob's justice and was left hanging from the tree. At some point, the white dog returned and stayed by the man's body.

In short order, facts came to light that cleared the peddler of the murder. Although proven wrong, the townspeople couldn't admit to their injustice and wouldn't even cut the man's corpse down. After a time, both the peddler's body and the dog disappeared.

But the town hadn't seen the last of the white dog. In 1855, plantation owner William Hardy sent a young boy out to retrieve a doctor to come treat a sick man on his property. The boy was riding a donkey down Old Buncombe Road when he heard a howl behind him. Looking back, the boy spotted a massive white dog. The boy sped up, but the hound gave chase, catching up and darting around in front of the donkey. The donkey reacted by rearing up, and the white dog vanished.

Once the boy made it to his destination, the residence of Dr. George Douglass, he told the doctor his tale. Being a man of science, the doctor brushed the story off and ignored it. But Dr. Douglass changed his mind when he later had his own experience and saw the ghostly dog himself.

The dog is said to be as large as a Saint Bernard with great speed and strength. Stories circulated that the hound would attack members of the mob that had killed the peddler. Oddly, the man who shot at the animal was never chased, but supposedly his four-year-old son vanished and was never seen again.

A man named Barry Sanders reported that the hound chased him in 1936. Sanders was on his way home when he spotted the dog staring at him. He ran screaming and the hound gave chase, not relenting until Sanders reached the edge of his own property which was apparently safe territory out of the hound's range.

The dog haunts a stretch of Old Buncombe Road deep in the Sumter National Forest, a path that was once a stagecoach route. The hound's territory is said to be between Ebenezer Church in Maybinton (formerly Maybinton Township) in Newberry County and Goshen Hill in Union County.

Nancy Roberts in *South Carolina Ghosts from the Coast to the Mountains* describes one man's experience trying to escape the fearsome hound:

"There, bounding along behind him, was a dog larger than any he had ever seen. The animal was close upon him, ready to spring. His heart leaped within him. He spun around and with all his strength brought the stick down full across the animal's face but to his astonishment felt no resistance at all. The stick had passed right through the beast's head and the slavering, gaping mouth and enormous eyes like balls of fire were still hurtling through the air toward him.

"He heard panting beside him, felt an icy pressure against his leg, and then came a howl so unearthly it seemed to emanate from the very depths of hell."

Robert's version is a typical ghostly tale that conveys the fear that many people reportedly experienced when encountering the ghost dog.

Another physician saw the white dog too; in fact, he spotted it on more than one occasion. Dr. Jim Coefield's sightings are not dated, but he reportedly saw the white hound as he was walking home with his own dog by his side. Coefield's dog ran off into the woods when the hound appeared, and the white beast followed Coefield home.

The doctor's dog returned home, but afterwards, refused to walk down Old Buncombe Road. Coefield was another man of science who didn't believe in ghosts, phantoms, or spirits of any kind but admitted that he could not explain what he saw.

A more terrifying experience with the hound was reported by an elderly woman in the 1970s. She saw the ghost hound standing at the edge of her yard. As she watched, the beast grew in size until it was massive, at which point it suddenly leapt toward her. The poor woman was so frightened that she fainted. When she came to, she quickly looked around, but there was no sign of the dog.

The legend of the Hound of Goshen may be just that—a legend. But many tales such as these have a foundation in at least some grains of truth. Perhaps there was some large, white animal roaming the woods that people connected with the local legend of the unjust murder.

We simply won't know unless, or until, someone has an even more dramatic encounter with a strange white beast near Goshen Hill.

Giant Snakes

A curious bit of lore from the town of York claims that a giant snake had taken up residence in the town and had lived there for over fifty years when the *Daily Gazette* out of Gastonia, North Carolina, reported on the story. The paper clearly thought the story was a fabrication but noted that the tale had been told for a long time in the area. According to the May 6, 1920, edition of the *Gazette*:

"There is a 50-year-old myth of a tremendous snake that makes its home on the lot on East Madison Street next to the municipal power house. Recently it was reported that a prominent citizen, while driving a car in broad daylight, encountered the snake crossing the road in the direction of the oil mill to which it was going in search of a dinner of rats. The snake was alleged to have been long enough to stretch entirely along the road with its body six inches through, and the prominent citizen, afraid to attempt to run over it, stopped until it had passed by. Investigation, however, failed to develop the slightest corroboration from the prominent citizen in question. It was the first time he had ever heard of the big snake. Although the fiction has persisted for at least 50 years, during all that time there has been found no reputable citizen who claims to have seen the reptile. Considering the age of the snake, it ought to be a large one; and considering the imaginary status of it, there is no reasonable limit as to its size."

One wonders how and why the story spread in the first place, but sadly, the origin of the serpentine tale seems to have been lost to time.

Other large snakes pop up on occasion in the Palmetto State. In the spring of 2012, Columbia resident Andrew Philson got a call from his elderly neighbor who reported a large snake in the back yard of Philson's house. The man went out expecting a run of the mill black or garden snake, but he received a shock when he spotted a 15- to 20-foot-long reptile slithering up a tree in his yard.

Officials at the state's Department of Natural Resources told Philson that the snake was likely a common rat snake, but the Columbia man didn't buy the explanation, noting, "I've seen rat snakes and they don't get that big."

Philson believed the snake was some type of python and tried to find someone to remove the snake. "I think this is a public nuisance and I think people need to know in this area that there's a snake this big on the loose," Philson said.

Philson said he was keeping his three-year-old son out of the yard until the creature was caught. Some residents speculated that the snake might be an invasive python that had made its way up from Florida and points south.

Monkey Island

Morgan Island is an uninhabited island in Beaufort County, uninhabited by humans that is. The island does have a population of primates—somewhere in the neighborhood of four thousand rhesus monkeys. The colony of monkeys has led to the spot commonly being known as Monkey Island.

The story of the island's monkeys goes back to 1979 when a primate research center in La Parguera, Puerto Rico, had to shut down. The state of South Carolina offered Morgan Island, and 1400 monkeys were shipped to the state and set loose on the island.

The island is a 4,489-acre marshland island with 635 acres of upland. The breeding colony of monkeys are Indian origin rhesus monkeys and are free ranging on the land.

The island is owned and operated by the South Carolina Department of Natural Resources and the monkeys are owned by the US Food and Drug Administration.

On rare occasions, a monkey will somehow escape the island. In the early 2000s, one crossed the Morgan River and made its way to the Lady's Island Golf Course seven miles away.

Perhaps the monkey was curious, or perhaps it was trying to escape; after all, the monkeys are used by the government as test subjects in the study of biological attacks and the study of infectious diseases.

Monkey Island is listed as restricted access and off limits to the public, although it may be possible to get permission to visit with authorized personnel. Alternatively, if you have access to a boat, it's possible to see the monkeys, though approaching too close to the island is also not allowed.

There are plenty of monkeys on the island, but not in other areas of the state, at least not officially. Still, York County reportedly has some unusual monkeys that appear from time to time, and they seem to be of a more ghostly variety.

Monkey Island

White Beasts of York County

White Wolf Hollow, near the town of Bethany, is known as a strange place. It lies between a pair of ridges that form part of the eastern slopes of Kings Mountain.

Reportedly, the place was named after white wolves that used to live in the area. While the wolves are long gone, there are frequent sightings of other white animals; deer, racoons, even large white panthers have been reported in the area. But most startling, perhaps, are the white monkeys.

Hunters out for deer in the region say they've been shocked to see white monkeys suddenly leap out of the brush. Often this occurs when people are driving at night and the unusual animal gets illuminated by the vehicle headlights. Even more shocking, the monkeys appear so suddenly and so close that drivers often think they'll hit them, but the creatures vanish before there is an impact.

Those who research the supernatural have pointed out that Kings Mountain itself contains a lot of oddly pale local fauna. The region seems to have a lot of unusual qualities. Reportedly, homing pigeons have been known to lose their bearings if they fly near the crest of the ridge. Some theories suggest that the mountain has large deposits of quartz crystal, iron, and lithium which may affect the area's magnetic field. Others point to ghostly legends associated with the mountain, including a battle during the American Revolution that left over 150 dead on the mountain battlefield.

Whatever the case, one thing is sure, there are strange things to be found in White Wolf Hollow.

Boo Hags

Imagine this. You wake up one morning, prepared to take on the day, but quickly find that it's a struggle to get dressed and moving. Shaking off the tired as best as you can, you make your way to the coffee pot, thinking that your morning caffeine will help, but after three cups, you're still as tired as ever.

The pattern repeats the next morning, but seems even worse, and with each day, your level of exhaustion grows. A quick visit to the doctor gives you no answers, and in a twist of irony, the physician suggests that you try to get "better rest."

The answer to your dilemma may not lie in the physical realm at all, but in the supernatural, for, according to Southern lore, you may well be the victim of a dreaded boo hag.

The legend of the boo hag comes to the South via the Gullah culture found along the southern coast. The Gullah, also known as the Geechee, are a unique cultural group who speak a Creole dialect of English.

Around half a million Gullah people live on the east coast from Florida up to North Carolina, with the highest concentration in South Carolina's Lowcountry region, especially on the state's Sea Islands.

Gullah culture is considered a product of the slave trade period when Africans, especially from West and Central Africa, were brought to the United States. Ayoka Campbell, in her introduction to *Gullah Cultural Legacies*, notes the distinct connection between the Gullah people and Africa:

"We are widely known as Gullahs and more esoterically as Geechees...there is a true connection between Gullah people and Africans who had never left the continent. We are descendants of enslaved people brought from Africa some 400 years ago, who have retained Africanisms in our speech, food ways, and daily ways of living."

Once they were thrown together in America, these diverse peoples created a blended cultural group with its own folklore, spiritual beliefs, and story-telling traditions.

Many traditions found on the Sea Islands are rooted in Gullah spiritual beliefs and offer a variety of ways to deal with various entities and spirits that are believed to exist in the region. The tradition of painting window frames, roofs, doorways, and porch frames blue is said to be a powerful ward against evil spirits. The color is even commonly known as "haint blue" in reference to "haints," or spirits. The tradition is likely rooted in the idea that spirits cannot cross water; hence, the watery color of blue offers a defense against them. But normal haints, or ghosts, are one thing. A more dreaded figure is the boo hag, a powerful supernatural creature that is considered deadly.

Emory S. Campbell notes in *Gullah Cultural Legacies* that boo hags, or "booga hags, are defined as "A person with unusual facial features, ugly; one who frightens as a Booga Hag."

Campbell further defines hags, noting: "The spirit of Hags is believed to attempt to smother certain people while they sleep at night."

But what exactly are these creatures? It's interesting to note that in the same book, Campbell defines "boogie man" as a "fictious character that produces fear" while the reality of hags and boo hags is listed simply without commentary on their potential real existence. This shouldn't be taken as overly superstitious on their part. Rather, it's a further reflection on how serious the Gullah consider the spiritual and supernatural world.

According to the Gullah spiritual view, humans have both a soul and a spirit. When a person dies, their soul leaves the body and journeys to heaven. At least, this is the case if the individual was good in life. A good person's spirit is the part that remains behind on earth to watch over family members as a sort of guardian angel.

People who aren't so good in life, well, their afterlife is a bit different. An evil person's soul takes the down escalator while their spirit remains on earth and carries out dark activities.

In short, the Gullah believe that people are going to behave in the afterlife much the way they did before they died. But it's a bit more complicated since these dark spirits can take the form of a number of different negative entities, like the boo hag.

Time and a mix of folktales have muddied the waters a bit in terms of some aspects of boo hags. While some stories indicated the creatures are former humans, other accounts seem to portray them as something akin to vampires, witches, or other evil entities. The reality is probably a combination somewhere in between.

The vampiric comparison is easy to understand when one realizes that boo hags thrive by feeding off the lifeforce of humans. They select a victim and wait until the person is sleeping, at which point, they "ride" the victim all night, stealing their breath and energy and slipping away just before dawn.

The attacks can stretch out for days, or even weeks, as the victim becomes more and more drained. Reportedly, being ridden by a boo hag makes a person slip into a dreamlike state, making it impossible for them to wake up and push the creature off. The following morning, the victim is extremely tired and "haggard," unable to go about their normal daily routines.

Boo hags are specific to Gullah culture, but similar hag lore can be found all over the world and includes the infamous succubus, a purported sexual demon that drains life force, as well as the more universal "hag," a nocturnal creature that feeds on the lifeforce of humans.

Modern science believes people suffering such effects are experiencing sleep paralysis, a state during which the person is unable to move or speak but may be aware of their surroundings. It's believed that people in such a state may also experience hallucinations.

Scientific explanations might work for some people, but others turn to the spiritual viewpoint, and the Gullah have given us a picture of the boo hag that is quite creepy.

According to the lore, the creatures are skinless and red in color with bulging blue veins. Some say they look like a human shaped piece of raw meat. When a boo hag is present, the room becomes very hot and damp. A terrible, rotting smell fills the air.

These nasty creatures can get into a home through even the smallest of openings: a door or window that's slightly open, a small crack, even a keyhole.

Boo hags appear like normal humans during the daylight hours. It's only at night that they are skinless, for they remove their skin in order to go out on their nocturnal hunt for energy. Shedding their skin makes the boo hag invisible.

The skins they wear during the day, well, those are said to be the skins of past victims. A skin is used until it wears out, at which point the hag simply steals another to use. The boo hag's skin suit is crucial, for it's said that if a hag is caught out in daylight without it, she will die.

Boo hags creep into the house and find a place to perch until they attack. Because of this, some people cut the bed post off their bed frames to eliminate a potential perch for the creatures. Others go so far as to remove things like lamps or other objects that may provide a perch for the dreaded things.

There's plenty of other defenses against boo hags, too. Reportedly, the creatures are a bit obsessive compulsive, particularly about numbers. Presented with certain items, the boo hag cannot help but stop and count. Brooms, hairbrushes, sieves, and kitchen colanders are common items that are hung on doors or near beds to distract the nasty creatures. When the hag spots such things, it cannot help but stop and count the bristles or holes so that it knows how many are there.

Some believe that if a Bible is out, the boo hag is compelled to read it from front to back, a time-consuming process that would cause them to run out of time to attack their victim.

Some hags can count quickly, so it's thought that leaving multiple items nearby for them to count provides a greater level of protection.

The list of defenses against the creatures seems to go on and on: a broom standing in the corner, seeds scattered around windows, a fork under the pillow.

Reportedly, if an old horseshoe is hanging over the door, the boo hag will be forced to travel every mile that the horse traveled.

They also hate salt, and some suggest keeping a container of it by the bedside. Some say the hags will count grains of salt. Others say that if salt is thrown on the hag, it causes them tremendous pain and burns them.

According to other lore, the smell of burning candles will keep hags away, so those afraid of boo hags often have numerous candles burning in their homes at night.

Laying a loaded shotgun across the head of the bed is also said to be a defense against the nocturnal attackers, though this seems like it could lead to other dangers, especially for someone who is a restless sleeper. The reasoning for this defense is that hags are said to detest the smell of gunpowder. On that note, rubbing gunpowder on cracks and openings in the home will keep the nasty things out.

Some people claim that if your willpower is strong enough, you can grab a boo hag when it is riding you. This is a risky move, but reportedly, if you are successful, the boo hag will flee and never plague you again.

One of the most popular defenses against boo hags is the use of the color indigo blue, or "haint blue." Painting window frames and doors with the color is said to repel the dark creatures and prevent them from entering homes.

If a boo hag's skin is found while she is out of it, there are two things that can be done. The skin can be filled with salt, so that when the boo hag dons it, she is burned and gravely injured. Others claim the hag's skin can be pitched into a fire and burned, leaving the creature nothing to return to. As a result, the boo hag is unable to resume her daytime life.

Sometimes, however, home defenses simply aren't enough, and the boo hag's victim needs professional help to defeat the entity. In such worst-case scenarios, a root doctor is sought out to get rid of the hag. A conjuror, or root doctor, has various methods to capture the creatures. The conjuror will sit in the victim's room at night while the person sleeps and wait for the hag to show up. At the first signs of the boo hag's presence, the root doctor opens a mason jar filled with pins and needles. He waves the jar over the victim while speaking a spell. The hag is captured in the jar and the jar is sealed and buried. The captured hag—separated from its skin—dies a slow and horrible death, and is left "sitting on pins and needles" for eternity.

In the past, old women were often pointed to as possibly being boo hags, but conversely there's an old saying that even the most beautiful girl in the world might actually be a boo hag.

One South Carolina native told me "The gorgeous girl next door might be a boo hag, or your mother-in-law might be a boo hag." No doubt, many people would confirm their mother-in-law is an evil entity.

Occasionally, modern accounts from those suffering from sleep paralysis and/or the hag phenomenon are connected to boo hag lore. One curious online posting came from a man who believes he may have encountered one of the creatures while on a trip to South Carolina. He writes:

"I just got back home from a business trip to Hilton Head Island. I'm not one to have nightmares hardly ever, but every night I slept there I had very dark dreams with demonic type spirit/ghost undertones. I did some research on Gullah legends and came across the boo hag. I never had any type of sleep paralysis while there and thank God never have. The last night I put the brooms from the condo in the corner of the room and I slept without any bad dreams at all."

Coincidence or something more?

While the boo hag may sound like a creature of pure folklore, it's important to note that for the people of South Carolina's Sea Islands, the creatures are very, very real, and stories of them have been passed down through countless generations. So, if you're ever in the region, just remember the popular saying— "Don't let the boo hag ride ya!"

Boo Hags

Plat Eyes

Boo hags aren't the only thing reportedly creeping around South Carolina's Lowcountry at night. Equally creepy are the dreaded "plat-eyes."

According to some tales, the creatures have a single, large red eye in the middle of their heads, "round as a plate" and a possible source of the creature's unusual name. But, as they say, don't count on descriptions of the creature to be accurate, for they can shape shift at will.

Plat-eyes are able to assume the form of a cat, dog, owl, or other domestic or wild animals. They can also appear in the form of a human apparition or even as a billowing, shapeless black cloud.

It's said that when a plat-eye shifts into another form, it can never do so perfectly, something is always "off." They may, for example, appear as a dog that has been run over by a truck, or as a misshapen pig. Whatever the case, something is always "wrong" with the picture.

This curious aspect is similar to the Christian belief that demons can manifest in earthly and even human form, but not perfectly—something, some part of the body, is always misshapen.

Plat-eyes are said to be abundant in the Palmetto State's Lowcountry and are especially active during the full moon. It's said they like to hang around graveyards as well as the swamps, woods, fields, and less-developed areas of the Lowcountry which provide them ample space to lurk.

One thing is sure; at night, the Lowcountry region takes on a different, haunting quality and it's easy to imagine something strange and unknown hiding in the darkness.

There are tales of travelers making their way home through the woods and swamps who encounter plat-eyes. Reportedly, the first sign of a potential encounter with one of the creatures is the sighting of a known animal. Often, the animal is larger than its kind would normally be, or it may have glowing eyes or appear ghostly white in color.

Such a sighting is followed by an encounter with a larger animal of equal strangeness, then yet another even larger animal. The unnerving encounters send people fleeing in the darkness hoping to escape.

Plat-eyes can also show up in people's homes and some say that root doctors or conjurers can control the spirits, directing them to punish those that have been targeted by the conjurer's clients.

The creatures will reportedly drive people to insanity and can do so simply by manifesting and harassing a person. An article in the February 8, 1970, edition of Columbia, SC, paper *The State* mentions plat-eyes showing up at people's homes. The paper reported:

"The plat-eye, as the story goes, manifests itself as a little kitten which scratches at people's doors at dusk. If he is let in, another kitten, this one a little larger, begins to scratch at the door. In succession, larger and larger cats come to the door and a supernatural force compels the host to let them in. By midnight, the house is filled with cats, some of them as big as tigers, who roam the house all night."

Plat-eyes are reportedly people who died and were never buried properly. Some say that many of them in South Carolina are the spirits of pirates who were beheaded for their crimes and left to rot, never having been blessed or interred. Legends say the bodies of these men were often tossed into the swamp or ocean. Such poor afterlife treatment made the spirits angry, and they transformed into the vengeful plat-eyes.

In some cases, plat-eyes are said to guard over treasures buried in the distant past, a spectral guardian that ensures no one disturbs the forgotten riches.

This version of the creature seems to have become more

prominent after the Civil War when rumors of Confederate gold protected by the spirits of murdered slaves spread around the South.

Bert Lunan mentions the treasure connection to plat-eyes in the April 18, 1962, edition of Columbia's newspaper *The State*. Lunan writes:

"But the plat-eye...just don't go looking for buried treasure. The plat-eye develops when a dead man's head is buried with gold or silver. You go looking for the loot and out of the ground rises a six-legged calf or maybe a headless hog."

In some contexts, the creatures seem to operate as a sort of bogeyman to frighten children and keep them from wandering off into the woods alone. Other versions of the plat-eye legend paint them as vengeful entities, the spirits of those who have been murdered and seek revenge for their deaths.

But plat-eyes are not simply ghosts. They are said to have real, physical form. One interesting account was collected in the 1930s and details a woman's encounter with one of the dreadful creatures.

In the 1930s, during the Great Depression, the United States Government commissioned the Federal Writer's Project (FWP) as part of their effort to assist unemployed writers. During a two-year period, Genevieve W. Chandler took advantage of the government financing and interviewed over a hundred people in South Carolina's Lowcountry. Chandler collected many fascinating stories and recollections, and one is of interest here.

In May 1936, Addie Knox, a Gullah woman, told Chandler about her encounter with a plat-eye. Some find the original account difficult to read since it was written semi-phonetically. The *Carolina Conjure* website relates the details of the tale:

"Addie Knox describes how while walking home one evening around dusk she passes by a graveyard and enters into the dark woods nearby. At one point she comes upon a fallen cypress tree blocking her path on top of which a bull frog is sitting. Addie explains that she sees the frog turn into a series of animals that get progressively larger, including a cooter (turtle), and a black cat. Addie strikes the plat-eye with a stick several times and runs away as the plat-eye chases after her, getting bigger and bigger. She is finally able to get away from the dreaded spirit by showing no fear and trusting in God."

Addie Knox may have used the Lord's Prayer, which some believe is a good protection against the creatures. There are other defenses, too. Plat-eyes are said to be fond of whiskey—a good excuse to keep a flask on hand for protection. A bit of the alcohol poured on the ground will catch their attention and they will rush to drink it up, thus holding them until you can escape the scene and reach safety.

A mixture of gunpowder and sulfur is said to ward the creatures off, and the combination is often carried in a small burlap sack in a pocket or worn on one's person.

Just like with other creatures in the Lowcountry, plat-eyes can be repelled by the color haint blue, so having doorways, porch floors, window frames and other portions of the home painted with the color will ward them off.

But for those who believe, they say the best way to protect yourself from plat-eyes is simple—avoid being out in the woods after dark!

The horseshoe at the University of South Carolina.

Third Eye Man

Universities seem to be hotspots for tales of ghosts and hauntings, weird urban legends, and strange lore. Perhaps it's the unique atmosphere created by the yearly influx of young people fresh out of high school being thrust into a new world of higher learning, self-sufficiency, and a different level of stress and deadlines. Or maybe it's the locations themselves. After all, many campuses are a collection of majestic buildings with decades of history and, in many cases, connections to significant historic figures. Whatever the case, it's easy to find stories of various specters and sometimes bizarre figures. A prime example of this is the unique lore found at the University of South Carolina where the underground-dwelling Third-Eye Man lives.

The University is a prestigious school with a long and illustrious history. Founded in 1801 as the College of South Carolina, the campus was closed during the American Civil War and converted into a military hospital during the conflict. After the war, in 1866, the facility resumed operations as an institute of higher learning as the University of South Carolina (USC).

USC is renowned for having the largest Ernest Hemingway collection in the world, and the largest Robert Burns and Scottish literature collection outside of Scotland.

The University's campus covers over 359 acres in downtown Columbia and includes the historic horseshoe district on its main campus.

Like many cities, Columbia has a series of underground tunnels that run beneath various buildings around the city. This series of tunnels is reportedly composed of three primary sets that are all connected and pass beneath historic buildings such as the Governor's Mansion, the State House, and of course, the

University.

The first recorded account of the University's weird figure is from November 12, 1949. Christopher Nichols and another student were walking near the historic Longstreet Theatre. What was likely a normal fall night ended up taking a strange turn at 10:43 when the boys spotted an odd man dressed in silver. As the boys watched, the man pried open a manhole cover at the corner of Sumter and Green streets, climbed down into the sewer, and pulled the manhole cover back into place behind him.

Nichols was a writer for the University's newspaper, the *Gamecock*, (currently published as *The Daily Gamecock*). Thinking the bizarre sighting was a worthy news item, Nichols wrote an article about the figure he dubbed "the Sewer Man." The weird tale created interest for a few weeks, but then faded away. People started to assume that the boys had spotted a homeless person or made the story up completely. But the weird figure soon resurfaced.

Late in the evening on April 7, 1950, a police officer patrolling the campus spotted something on the ground on the loading docks at the Longstreet Theatre. Investigating closer, the officer found the mutilated remains of two chickens.

Disgusted at the sight, the policeman returned to his car and radioed the station to report the find. When he returned to the scene, he was surprised to see a man at the site. The figure was dressed in silver and was bent over one of the chicken carcasses.

The policeman brought his flashlight up and put the man in the spotlight, at which point he received an even bigger shock. The man's face was oddly colored and disfigured. Even more startling, in the center of the man's forehead was a third eye.

The officer rushed back to his patrol car and called for backup. By the time additional officers arrived, the strange man had vanished and all they found were the bones and feathers of the mutilated chickens.

Once he calmed down, the policeman who had spotted the man gave his account to his fellow officers. As would be expected, they didn't believe his story and thought that he had imagined the unusual details of the man's features.

Reportedly, the police officer stuck to his story, repeating it over the years even though many didn't believe the tale.

The account was quickly connected to the Sewer Man report, and the lore of what was now dubbed the "Third Eye Man" began to grow.

Of course, it's only natural that college students would make their way to the tunnels, or the "catacombs," as they're collectively known. Over the years, students used the underground passages for a range of activities, especially ones they would rather keep from the eyes of teachers and University administrators.

The added allure of a weird creature, or whatever it was, living in the tunnels added another dimension to the mysterious catacombs. It wasn't long before fraternities came up with the idea of taking pledges down into the tunnels as part of their hazing rituals.

Most of these journeys resulted in nothing more than some minor scares, but that changed in the late 1960s when the next significant encounter with the Third Eye Man took place.

It was an October night when a group of frat boys took three pledges down into the catacombs for an initiation ritual.

Rounding a corner in one of the tunnels, the boys suddenly saw what they thought was a crippled old man dressed in silver step out of the shadows of the tunnel. The weird figure was holding a pipe and was clearly ready to attack. He, or it, quickly charged the boys.

The frat brothers ran screaming from the tunnels but not before one of the pledges was knocked down by the attacker. The young man managed to escape and received only minor scrapes and bruises.

The police were contacted, and a search was made of the tunnels, but the Third Eye Man had once again vanished into the depths of the underworld maze.

It wasn't long before the University took measures to limit

access to the catacombs. Most of the entryways were sealed off entirely and only a small number of openings were left for maintenance purposes, but even maintenance workers at the site admit that they only venture into the tunnels if absolutely necessary. Whether this is due to the legend of the Third Eye Man or other reasons is unclear.

Some people claim that the University knows about the existence of the Third Eye Man and has covered up the story. At the least, USC officials don't encourage discussion of the tale and, in fact, seem to look down on questions about the topic. Entrance to the tunnels is strictly controlled and reportedly, those who violate the rule and venture into the catacombs can face suspension and even legal prosecution.

Over the years, various investigators have tried to gain permission to enter the tunnels and look for evidence of the Third Eye Man, but they are inevitably denied any official sanction to do so. University officials often note that the tunnels are sealed off for "safety reasons."

Of course, not everyone abides by the rules and according to both local lore and online postings, people have made their way into the catacombs on occasion, though no confirmed sightings of the Third Eye Man have been recorded.

Until or unless he chooses to step out of the shadows again, those of us who are curious about such things are left to wonder, does the strange Third Eye Man still lurk in the tunnels beneath Columbia?

PALMETTO STATE MONSTERS by David Weatherly

Acknowledgements

Thanks to all my friends, colleagues, and family who continue to support my work and provide invaluable assistance. They include Lyle Blackburn, John LeMay, Loren Coleman, Dr. Jeff Meldrum, Chad Lewis, Ken Gerhard, Nick Redfern, Kevin Nelson, Micha Hanks, Joshua P. Warren, Sam Shearon, Josh Turner, Jay Bachochin, Doug Hajicek, Paul Bestall, Joshua Cutchin, Bruce Champagne, and Sherman Carmichael.

A very special thanks to South Carolina cryptid researcher Mike Richburg for sharing his insights and personal accounts for this volume.

Thanks to all the witnesses and organizations who provided information and data about sightings and experiences detailed in this volume.

PALMETTO STATE MONSTERS by David Weatherly

Bibliography

Bennett, John. Doctor to the Dead: Grotesque Legends & Folk Tales of Old Charleston. Rinehart & Company, New York, NY. 1943.

Bennett, John. The Treasure of Peyre Gaillard Being an Account of the Recovery, on a South Carolina Plantation of a Treasure. The Century Company, New York, NY. 1906.

Berry, Rick. Bigfoot on the East Coast. Self-published. 1993.

Blackburn, Lyle. Lizard Man: The True Story of the Bishopville Monster. Anomalist Books, San Antonio, TX. 2013.

Campbell, Emory S. Gullah Cultural Legacies. Gullah Heritage Consulting Services, Hilton Head Island, SC. 2008.

Carmichael, Sherman. Legends and Lore of South Carolina. The History Press, Charleston, SC. 2012.

Carmichael, Sherman. Mysterious South Carolina. History Press, Charleston, SC. 2019.

Carmichael, Sherman. Strange South Carolina. History Press, Charleston, SC. 2015.

Coleman, Loren and Clark, Jerome. Creatures on the Outer Edge. Warner Books, New York, NY. 1978.

Crowe, Ray. Bigfoot Behavior Volume II. CreateSpace Independent Publishing, Scotts Valley, CA. 2015.

Crowe, Ray. Bigfoot Behavior Volume III. CreateSpace Independent Publishing, Scotts Valley, CA. 2015.

Heuvelmans, Bernard. In the Wake of Sea Serpents. Hill & Wang, New York, NY 1969.

Lawson, John. A New Voyage to Carolina. University of North Carolina Press, Chapel Hill, NC. 1967.

LeMay, John. Southerners & Saurians: Swamp Monsters, Lizard Men, and Other Curious Creatures of the Old South. Bicep Books. 2020.

Manley, Roger. Weird Carolinas: Your Travel Guide to North and South Carolina's Local Legends and Best Kept Secrets. Sterling Publishing, New York, NY 2007.

Mayes, Michael. Shadow Cats: The Black Panthers of North America. Anomalist Books, San Antonio, TX. 2018.

Mooney, James. History, Myths and Sacred Formulas of the Cherokees. Bright Mountain Books, Fairview, NC 1992.

Orr, Bruce. Ghosts of Berkeley County, South Carolina. Haunted America a Division of History Press, Charleston, SC. 2011.

Parson, Elsie Clews. Folk-Lore of the Sea Islands-South Carolina. American Folk-Lore Society, Bloomington, IN. 1923.

Rhyne, Nancy. Tales of the South Carolina Low Country. John F. Blair, Winston-Salem, NC. 1982.

Rife, Philip. Bigfoot Across America. Writers Club Press, Lincoln, NE 2000.

Roberts, Nancy. South Carolina Ghosts From the Coast to the Mountains. University of South Carolina Press, Columbia, SC. 1983.

Roffe, Denise. Ghosts and Legends of Charleston, South Carolina. Schiffer Publishing, Atglen, PA. 2010.

Magazines

Fate Magazine

South Carolina Wildlife Magazine.

Websites

BFRO (Bigfoot Field Researchers Organization)

Bigfoot Encounters

Carolina Conjure

GCRBO (Gulf Coast Bigfoot Researchers Organization).

Jeff Rense Sightings Website

Photo Credits

Scape Ore swamp, Lizard Man track, and Liston Truesdale photos courtesy of Lyle Blackburn.

All other photos by David Weatherly or are held in the public domain.

About the Author

David Weatherly

David Weatherly is a renaissance man of the strange and supernatural. He has traveled the world in pursuit of ghosts, cryptids, UFOs, magic, and more. From the specters of dusty castles, to remote, haunted islands, from ancient sites, to modern mysteries, he has journeyed to the most unusual places on the globe seeking the unknown.

David became fascinated with the paranormal at a young age. Ghost stories and accounts of weird creatures and UFOs led him to discover many of his early influences. Writers such as John Keel, Jacques Vallee, Hans Holzer and others set him on course to spend his life exploring and investigating the unexplained.

Throughout his life, he's also delved into shamanic and magical traditions from around the world, spending time with elders from numerous cultures in Europe, the Americas, Africa and Asia. He has studied with Taoist masters in China, Tibetan Lamas, and other mystics from the far east. He's picked up knowledge from African and Native American tribal elders and sat around fires with shamans from countless other traditions.

Along his path, David has also gathered a lot of arcane knowledge, studying a range of ancient arts from palmistry, the runes, and other obscure forms of divination, to alchemy and magick. He has studied and taught Qigong and Ninjutsu, as well as various energy related arts. David has also studied stage and performance magic.

His shamanic and magical background has given him a unique perspective in his explorations into the unknown, and he continues to write, travel, and explore, leaving no stone unturned in his quest for the strange and unusual.

David has investigated, and written about, a diverse range of topics, including, Hauntings & Ghosts, Cryptozoology, Ufology, Ancient Mysteries, Shamanism, Magic, and Psychic Phenomena.

David is the founder of the independent media and publishing company, Eerie Lights Publishing.

He has been a featured speaker at conferences around the world and has lectured for countless paranormal and spiritual groups.

He is a frequent guest on Coast to Coast AM with George Noory, Spaced Out Radio and other radio programs. David has also appeared on numerous television shows including the Travel Channel's Mysteries of the Outdoors, History Channel's Ancient Aliens, Beyond Belief and other programs. He was also featured in the highly successful series On The Trail of UFOs.

David's books include Strange Intruders, Eerie Companions, and the Monsters of America series.

Find David online at:

https://eerielights.com

Made in the USA
Las Vegas, NV
15 August 2023

76156260R00129